3

CREDITS

Writing
Tom Dowd

Editorial Staff
Senior Editor
Donna Ippolito
Assistant Editor
Kent Stolt
Editorial Assisant
Geri Rebstock

Production Staff
Production Manager
Sam Lewis
Art Director
Jordan Weisman
Cover Art
Steve Venters
Cover Design
Jeff Laubenstein
Book Design
Jacob Lurch
Illustration
Karl Martin
Jeff Laubenstein
Steve Venters
Tim Bradstreet
Layout
Tara Gallagher

Published by
FASA Corporation
P.O. Box 6930
Chicago, IL 60680

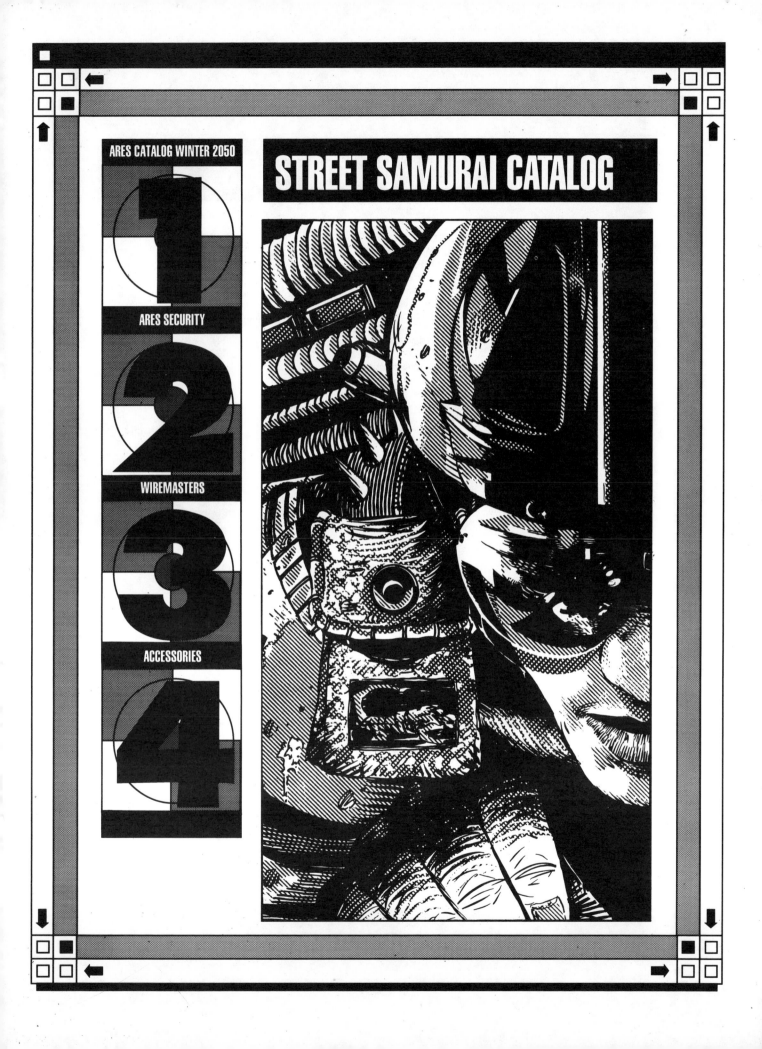

ARES CATALOG WINTER 2050

1

ARES SECURITY

2

WIREMASTERS

3

ACCESSORIES

4

STREET SAMURAI CATALOG

TABLE OF CONTENTS

ARES CATALOG WINTER 2050

1

ARES SECURITY

2

WIREMASTERS

3

ACCESSORIES

4

ARES WINTER CATALOG 2050

Our regular subscribers will notice quite a difference between this catalog and our last. As a direct result of input from our customers, we've been able to streamline enormously. We've taken their suggestions and transformed this catalog into a primary source for quality weapons and equipment. Every item on these pages has passed the most rigorous tests. That's why when you buy from Ares America, you know you're buying the best.

We've also begun the best money-back guarantee in the business. All our equipment has a flat 90-day warranty. No questions asked. On top of that, you still get our phenomenal 60 days or 1,000 rounds warranty on light firearms and 30 days or 10,000 rounds on heavy firearms. The best in the business, because you demanded it.

—Nathaniel Naidich, Director of Sales, Ares America

Ares America is a division of Ares Arms, a wholly owned subsidiary of Ares Macrotechnology Incorporated, Detroit Michigan, UCAS.

All items in this catalog are available, by special order, in a hypo-allergenic form for roughly 150 percent of the listed price.

>>>>>[Can you believe that guarantee drek, chummers? My buddy Wedge burned at least 20,000 rounds in his Valiant the first week he had it! Now admittedly, he's a bit intense…

As anyone can see, this is the current Ares catalog. Normally available only to subscribers, I've posted it here on the public databoard for all to see. Nothing super-special in this part, but just wait until you get to Section Two! (That's the part that's supposed to be available only to licensed police or security organizations with a valid credit rating.) The first part'll get you drooling, but Section Two will leave you wriggling on the floor.

This posted copy isn't protected, so feel free to comment as you like. All you jokers who read this, beware! I've got no control over who says what in this file once it's up, so not everything you read may be chip-truth. But then again, you never know….]<<<<<
—FastJack <14:34:27 10-07-50>

ORDER HERE

PAID

SALESPERSON

SECTION

1

ARES

MONOFILAMENT SWORD

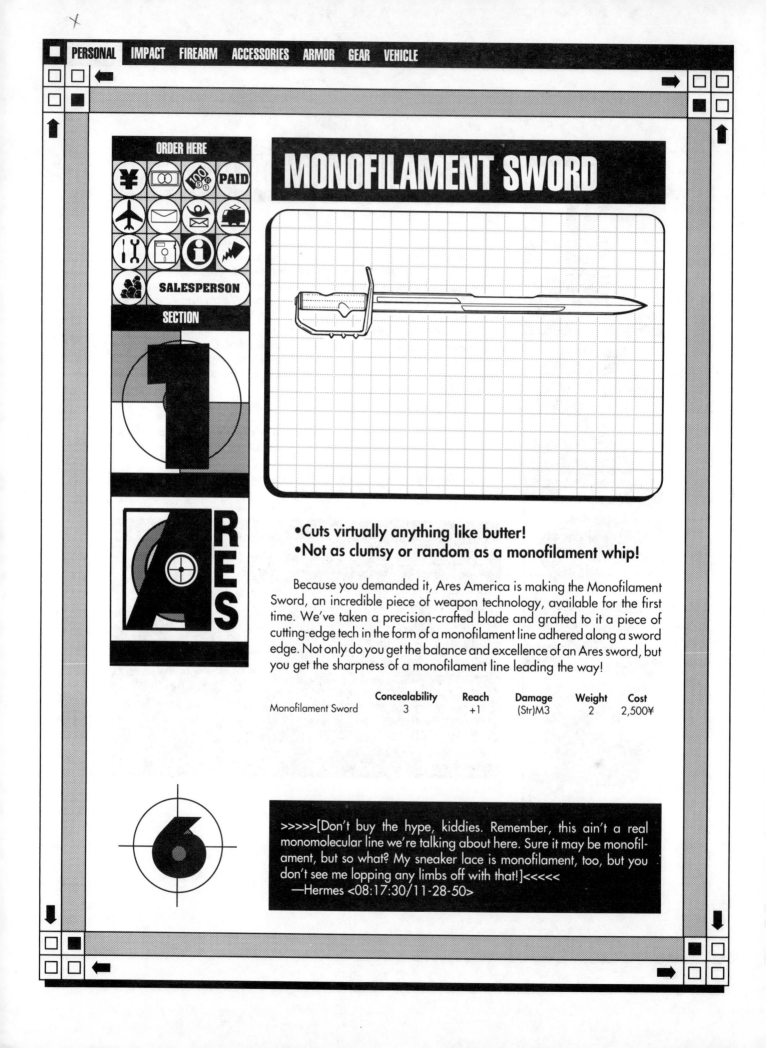

- •Cuts virtually anything like butter!
- •Not as clumsy or random as a monofilament whip!

Because you demanded it, Ares America is making the Monofilament Sword, an incredible piece of weapon technology, available for the first time. We've taken a precision-crafted blade and grafted to it a piece of cutting-edge tech in the form of a monofilament line adhered along a sword edge. Not only do you get the balance and excellence of an Ares sword, but you get the sharpness of a monofilament line leading the way!

	Concealability	Reach	Damage	Weight	Cost
Monofilament Sword	3	+1	(Str)M3	2	2,500¥

>>>>>[Don't buy the hype, kiddies. Remember, this ain't a real monomolecular line we're talking about here. Sure it may be monofilament, but so what? My sneaker lace is monofilament, too, but you don't see me lopping any limbs off with that!]<<<<<
—Hermes <08:17:30/11-28-50>

LASER CRESCENT AXE

ORDER HERE

SALESPERSON

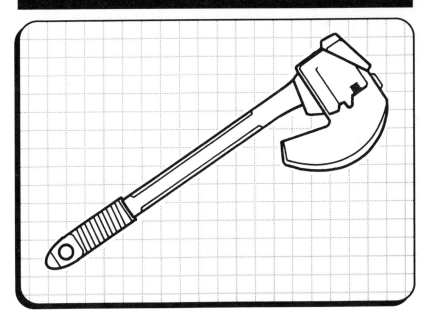

- **An industrial-strength, welding laser personal combat weapon!**
- **Safer than a monowhip and just as deadly!**

Here's one for Mr. Ripley. Designed by Centurion Industries for use against certain types of Awakened Critters, the Laser Crescent Axe carries a self-focusing, multi-track welding laser in a crescent-shaped mounting. The crescent shape keeps the weapon from snagging, and the laser ensures that there's nothing left to snag on! Literally on the cutting edge of technology!

	Concealability	Reach	Damage	Weight	Cost
Laser Axe	2	+1	(Str÷2)S2	5.2	3,500¥

>>>>>[Friend of mine had the opportunity to field-test this weapon, and though the effect is extreme, the odds in favor of knocking the laser out of alignment are pretty high. When he had it, the axe seemed to be down for repairs more often than it was working properly. Seemed that every third of fourth hit on armor knocked it out.]<<<<<
—Metallic Marauder <23:32:45/11-25-50>

ORDER HERE

SALESPERSON

SECTION

1

ARES

AZ-150 SUPER STUN BATON

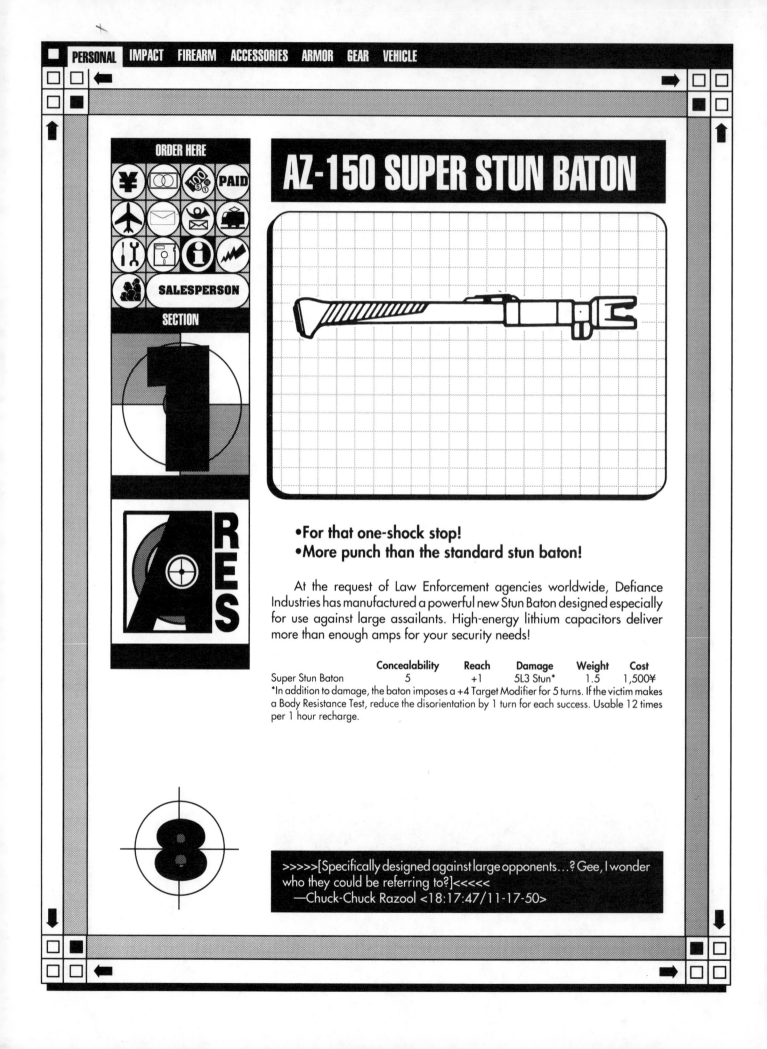

- •For that one-shock stop!
- •More punch than the standard stun baton!

At the request of Law Enforcement agencies worldwide, Defiance Industries has manufactured a powerful new Stun Baton designed especially for use against large assailants. High-energy lithium capacitors deliver more than enough amps for your security needs!

	Concealability	Reach	Damage	Weight	Cost
Super Stun Baton	5	+1	5L3 Stun*	1.5	1,500¥

*In addition to damage, the baton imposes a +4 Target Modifier for 5 turns. If the victim makes a Body Resistance Test, reduce the disorientation by 1 turn for each success. Usable 12 times per 1 hour recharge.

>>>>>[Specifically designed against large opponents…? Gee, I wonder who they could be referring to?]<<<<<
—Chuck-Chuck Razool <18:17:47/11-17-50>

8

FOREARM SNAP-BLADES

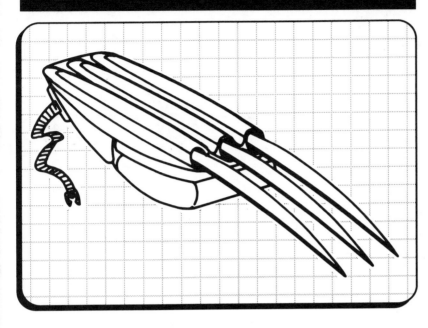

- •Cyberspurs, without the after-effects!
- •Muscle-triggered action!

Need that extra cyberspur edge, but can't afford the cost? Leetol Industries of Belgium has come up with the answer! These spur-blades are mounted in external forearm sheaths and respond to muscle-movement commands. POP!— they're out! SLITCHT!— they're retracted, and your opponent doesn't realize it until it's too late!

	Concealability	Reach	Damage	Weight	Cost
Snap-Blade	7	0	(Str)M2	1.5	850¥

>>>>>[Be careful with these, chummers. They don't come with the kind of bone reinforcing that real cyberspurs do, so watch out for those rotational and leverage-based moves when you've got resistance. Odds are a bone will snap before the blade does.]<<<<<
—Findler-Man <21:45:02/01-03-51>

ORDER HERE

SALESPERSON

SECTION

1

R
E
S

SURVIVAL KNIFE

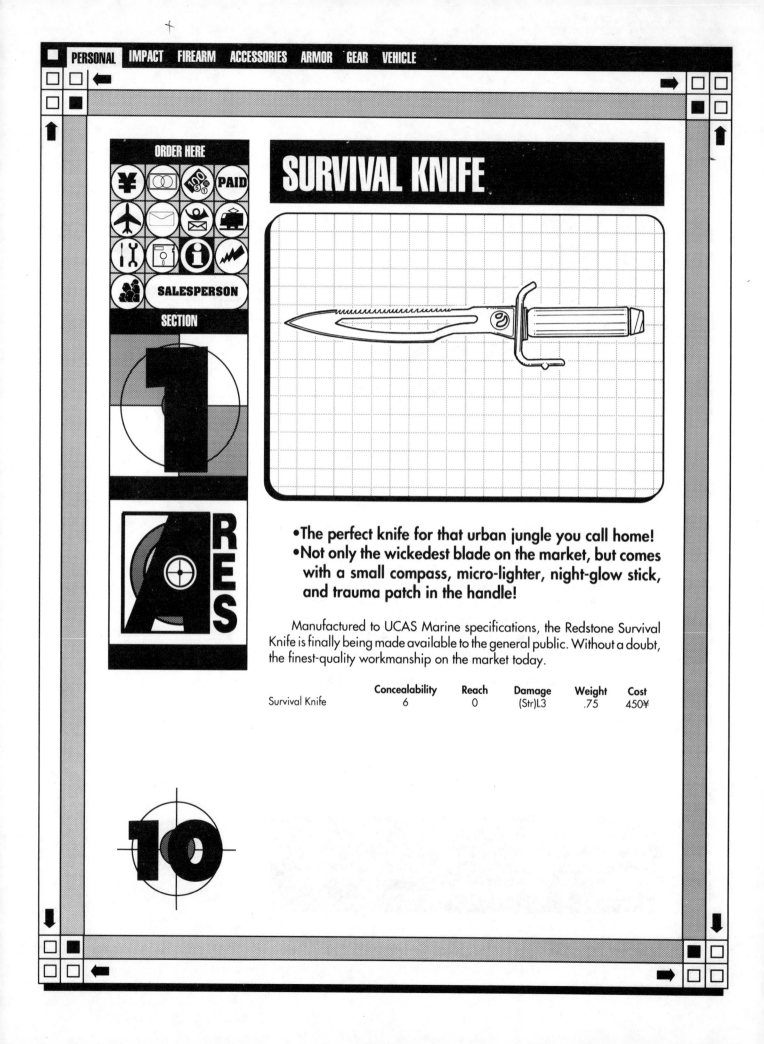

- **The perfect knife for that urban jungle you call home!**
- **Not only the wickedest blade on the market, but comes with a small compass, micro-lighter, night-glow stick, and trauma patch in the handle!**

Manufactured to UCAS Marine specifications, the Redstone Survival Knife is finally being made available to the general public. Without a doubt, the finest-quality workmanship on the market today.

	Concealability	Reach	Damage	Weight	Cost
Survival Knife	6	0	(Str)L3	.75	450¥

SHOCK GLOVE

- **Perfect for when the kid gloves come off and the nasty stuff goes on!**
- **Impact-triggered, it discharges only when you hit!**

Based on stun baton technology, the Reinco Shock Glove is a black, non-conducting plas-fabric interlaced with a partitioned wire mesh to provide the greatest chance for shock on impact. Flat battery/capacitors mount in a special vambrace for added convenience.

	Concealability	Reach	Damage	Weight	Cost
Shock Glove	9	0	5L3*	.5	950¥

*In addition to damage, this weapon imposes a +4 Target Modifier for 5 turns. If the victim makes a Body Resistance Test, reduce the disorientation by one turn for each success. Usable 8 times per 1 hour recharge. Fist damage reduced to(Str2)M1 when worn, and not usable with Hand Razors.

11

ORDER HERE

SALESPERSON

SECTION

1

ARES

COMBAT AXE

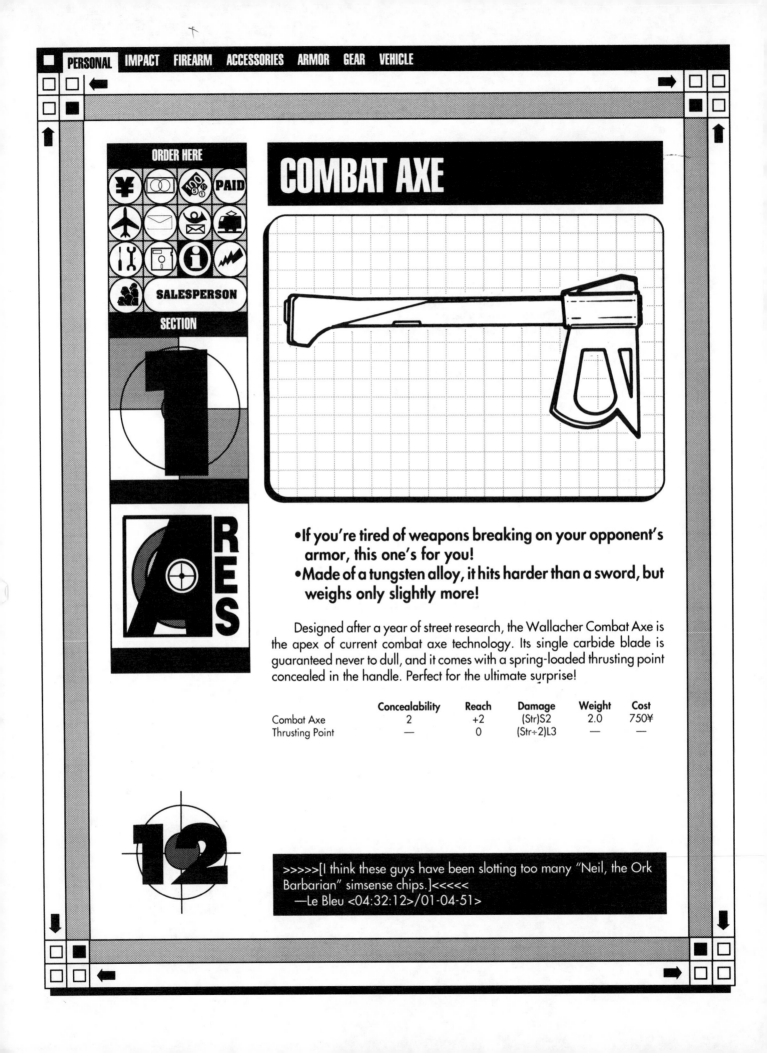

- If you're tired of weapons breaking on your opponent's armor, this one's for you!
- Made of a tungsten alloy, it hits harder than a sword, but weighs only slightly more!

Designed after a year of street research, the Wallacher Combat Axe is the apex of current combat axe technology. Its single carbide blade is guaranteed never to dull, and it comes with a spring-loaded thrusting point concealed in the handle. Perfect for the ultimate surprise!

	Concealability	Reach	Damage	Weight	Cost
Combat Axe	2	+2	(Str)S2	2.0	750¥
Thrusting Point	—	0	(Str÷2)L3	—	—

>>>>>[I think these guys have been slotting too many "Neil, the Ork Barbarian" simsense chips.]<<<<<
—Le Bleu <04:32:12>/01-04-51>

BOW ACCESSORY MOUNT

- **Allows the mounting of pistol accessories on your bow!**
- **Lightweight, yet durable!**

With this neat little gadget from Peterson Enterprises of Seattle, owners of various brands of bows can mount them with commonly available pistol accessories. Mountable accessories include laser sights, imaging scopes, and smartgun adapters.

	Concealability	Reach	Damage	Weight	Cost
Bow Accessory Mount	−1	—	—	+.1	100¥

13

ORDER HERE

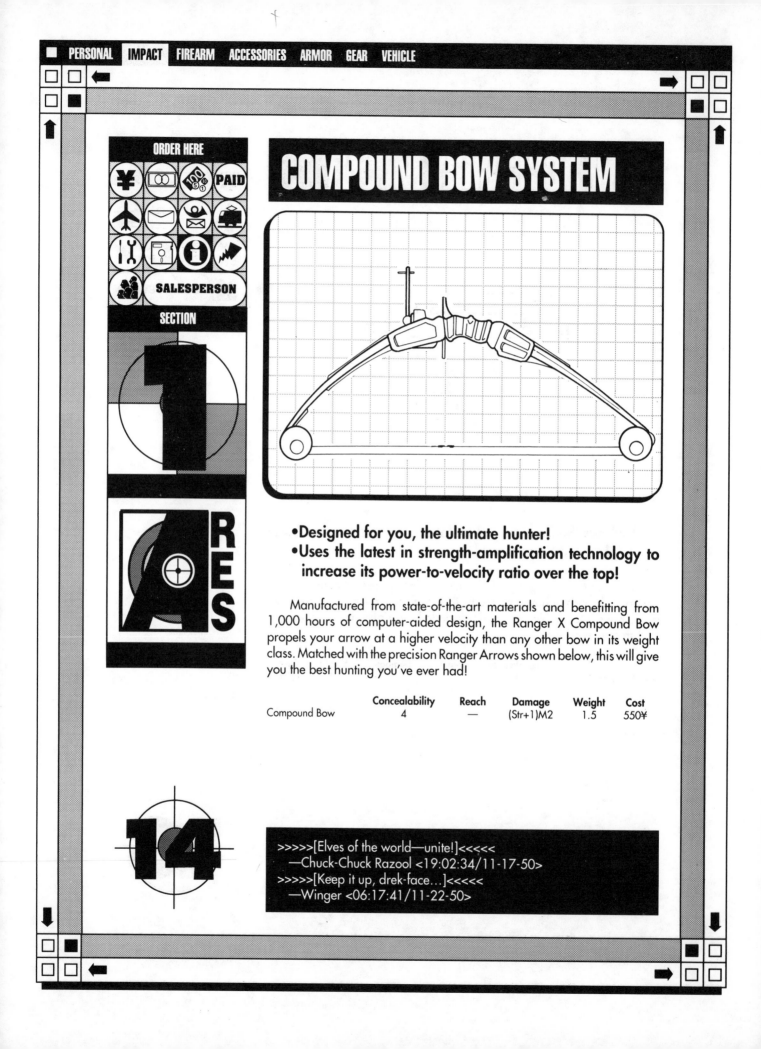

SALESPERSON

SECTION

1

ARES

COMPOUND BOW SYSTEM

- •Designed for you, the ultimate hunter!
- •Uses the latest in strength-amplification technology to increase its power-to-velocity ratio over the top!

Manufactured from state-of-the-art materials and benefitting from 1,000 hours of computer-aided design, the Ranger X Compound Bow propels your arrow at a higher velocity than any other bow in its weight class. Matched with the precision Ranger Arrows shown below, this will give you the best hunting you've ever had!

	Concealability	Reach	Damage	Weight	Cost
Compound Bow	4	—	(Str+1)M2	1.5	550¥

14

>>>>>[Elves of the world—unite!]<<<<<
—Chuck-Chuck Razool <19:02:34/11-17-50>
>>>>>[Keep it up, drek-face...]<<<<<
—Winger <06:17:41/11-22-50>

PRECISION ARROWS

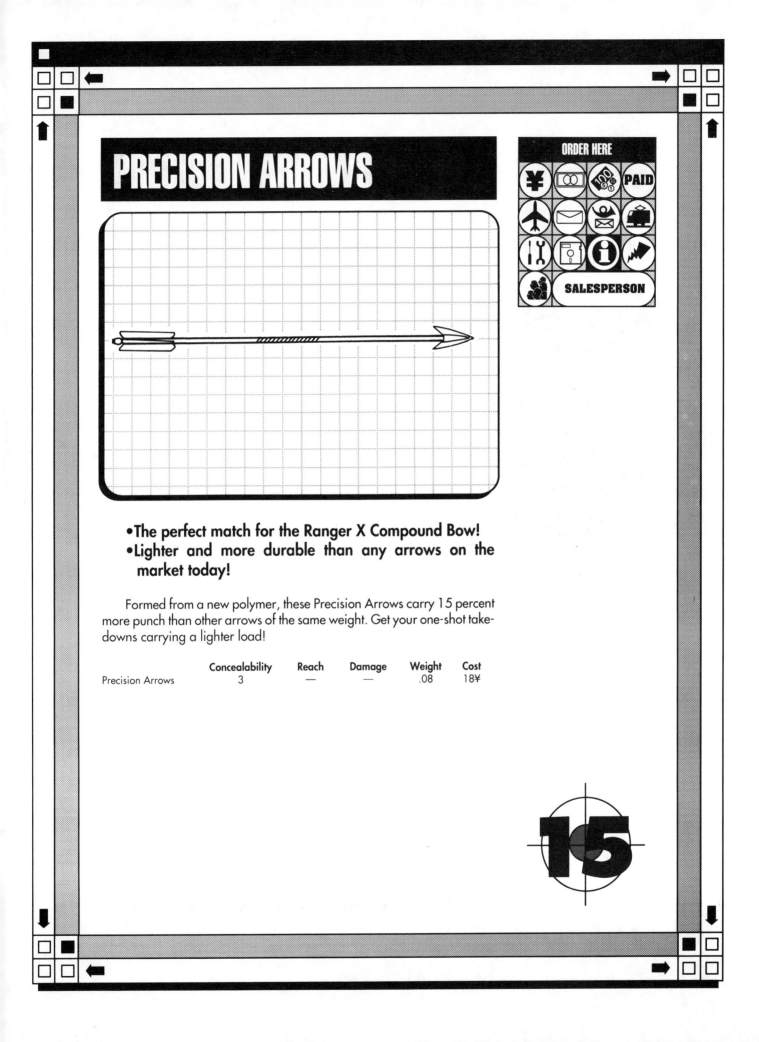

- **The perfect match for the Ranger X Compound Bow!**
- **Lighter and more durable than any arrows on the market today!**

Formed from a new polymer, these Precision Arrows carry 15 percent more punch than other arrows of the same weight. Get your one-shot take-downs carrying a lighter load!

	Concealability	Reach	Damage	Weight	Cost
Precision Arrows	3	—	—	.08	18¥

15

ORDER HERE

SALESPERSON

SECTION

1

ARES

CRUSADER MACHINE PISTOL

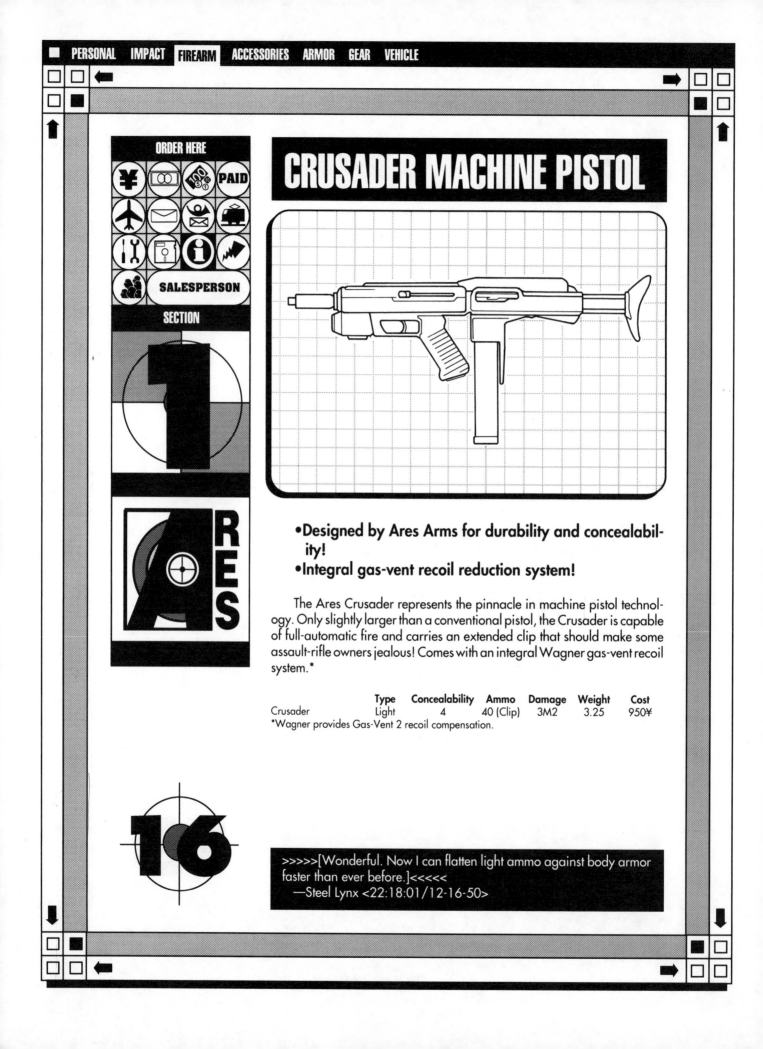

- •Designed by Ares Arms for durability and concealability!
- •Integral gas-vent recoil reduction system!

The Ares Crusader represents the pinnacle in machine pistol technology. Only slightly larger than a conventional pistol, the Crusader is capable of full-automatic fire and carries an extended clip that should make some assault-rifle owners jealous! Comes with an integral Wagner gas-vent recoil system.*

	Type	Concealability	Ammo	Damage	Weight	Cost
Crusader	Light	4	40 (Clip)	3M2	3.25	950¥

*Wagner provides Gas-Vent 2 recoil compensation.

16

>>>>>[Wonderful. Now I can flatten light ammo against body armor faster than ever before.]<<<<<
—Steel Lynx <22:18:01/12-16-50>

LIGHT FIRE 70

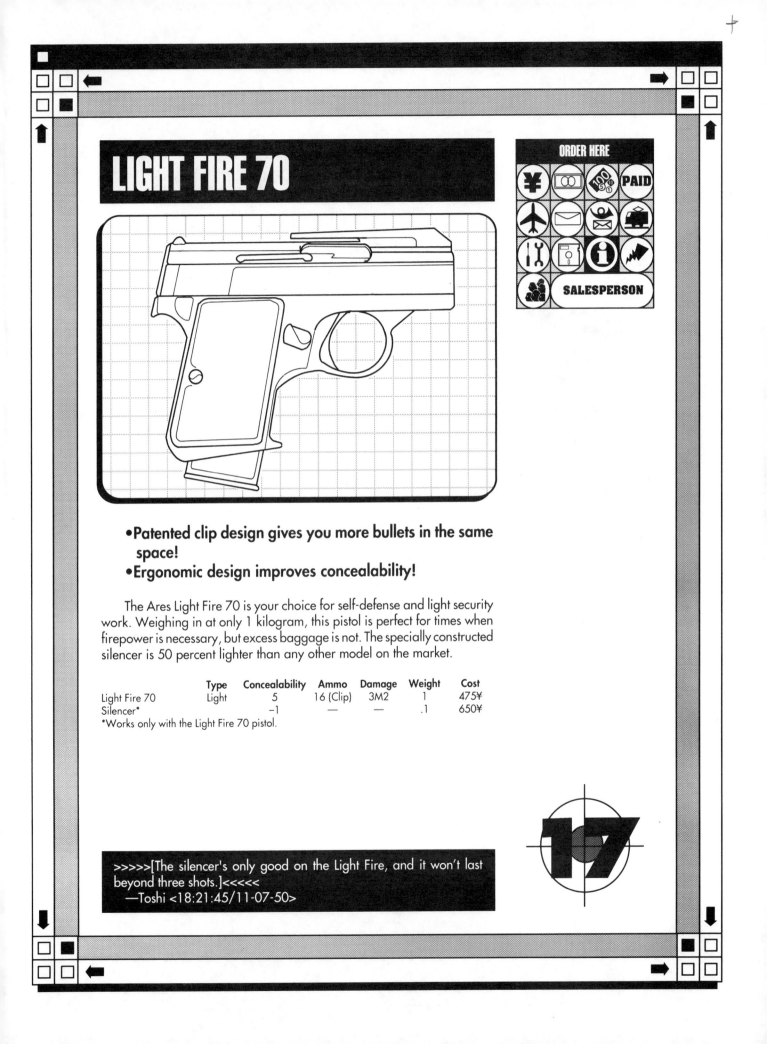

- **Patented clip design gives you more bullets in the same space!**
- **Ergonomic design improves concealability!**

The Ares Light Fire 70 is your choice for self-defense and light security work. Weighing in at only 1 kilogram, this pistol is perfect for times when firepower is necessary, but excess baggage is not. The specially constructed silencer is 50 percent lighter than any other model on the market.

	Type	Concealability	Ammo	Damage	Weight	Cost
Light Fire 70	Light	5	16 (Clip)	3M2	1	475¥
Silencer*		−1	—	—	.1	650¥

*Works only with the Light Fire 70 pistol.

>>>>>[The silencer's only good on the Light Fire, and it won't last beyond three shots.]<<<<<
—Toshi <18:21:45/11-07-50>

ORDER HERE

PAID

SALESPERSON

SECTION

1

A R E S

18

PREDATOR II

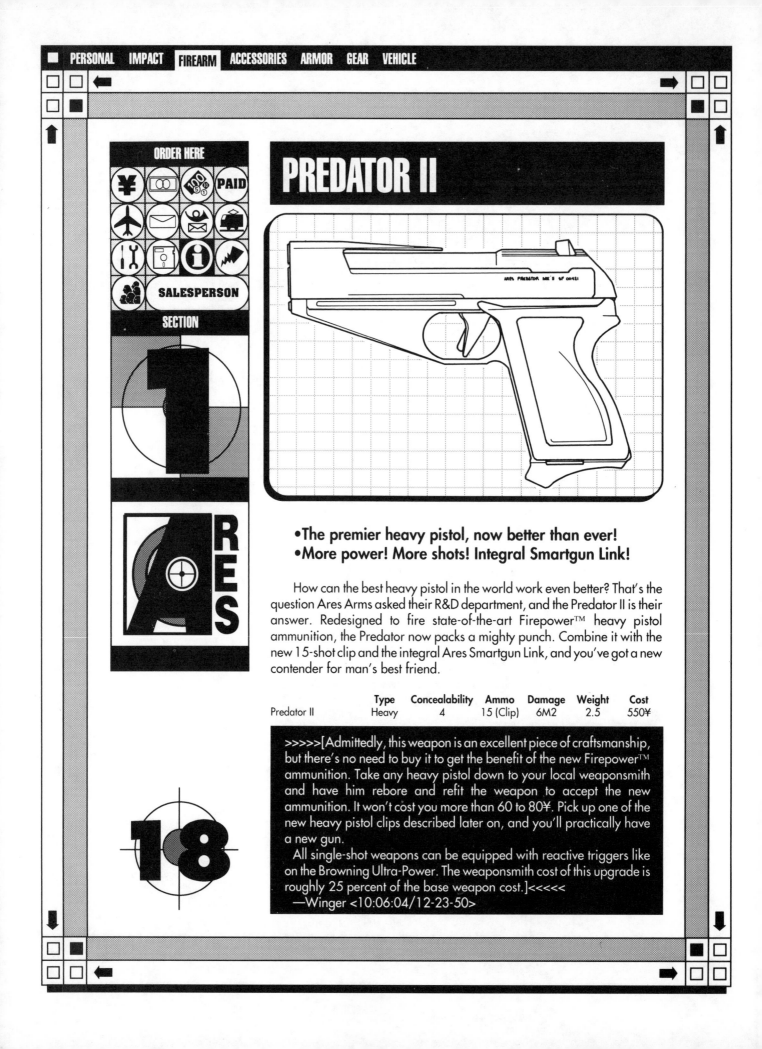

ARES PREDATOR MK II SF OH431

- •The premier heavy pistol, now better than ever!
- •More power! More shots! Integral Smartgun Link!

How can the best heavy pistol in the world work even better? That's the question Ares Arms asked their R&D department, and the Predator II is their answer. Redesigned to fire state-of-the-art Firepower™ heavy pistol ammunition, the Predator now packs a mighty punch. Combine it with the new 15-shot clip and the integral Ares Smartgun Link, and you've got a new contender for man's best friend.

	Type	Concealability	Ammo	Damage	Weight	Cost
Predator II	Heavy	4	15 (Clip)	6M2	2.5	550¥

>>>>>[Admittedly, this weapon is an excellent piece of craftsmanship, but there's no need to buy it to get the benefit of the new Firepower™ ammunition. Take any heavy pistol down to your local weaponsmith and have him rebore and refit the weapon to accept the new ammunition. It won't cost you more than 60 to 80¥. Pick up one of the new heavy pistol clips described later on, and you'll practically have a new gun.
   All single-shot weapons can be equipped with reactive triggers like on the Browning Ultra-Power. The weaponsmith cost of this upgrade is roughly 25 percent of the base weapon cost.]<<<<<
   —Winger <10:06:04/12-23-50>

BERETTA 200ST

- •Capable of full-automatic fire!
- •An incredible 26-shot magazine!
- •Redefines the concept of light service pistol!

The pistol that all the military data-faxes are screaming about. The Beretta Model 200ST is everything you've heard and more. Capable of full-automatic fire, this pistol jams as much firepower into a small frame as any other light service pistol currently available. Plus, the 26-shot magazine reduces the chance of being caught short at those critical moments. Equipped with detachable pistol shoulder-stock.*

	Type	Concealability	Ammo	Damage	Weight	Cost
Model 200ST	Light	4	26 (Clip)	3M2	2	700¥

*Shoulder Stock gives 1 point of Recoil Compensation. The maximum number of shots in autofire is 4, regardless of Firearms Skill Rating.

19

ORDER HERE

SALESPERSON

SECTION

1

RES

ULTRA-POWER

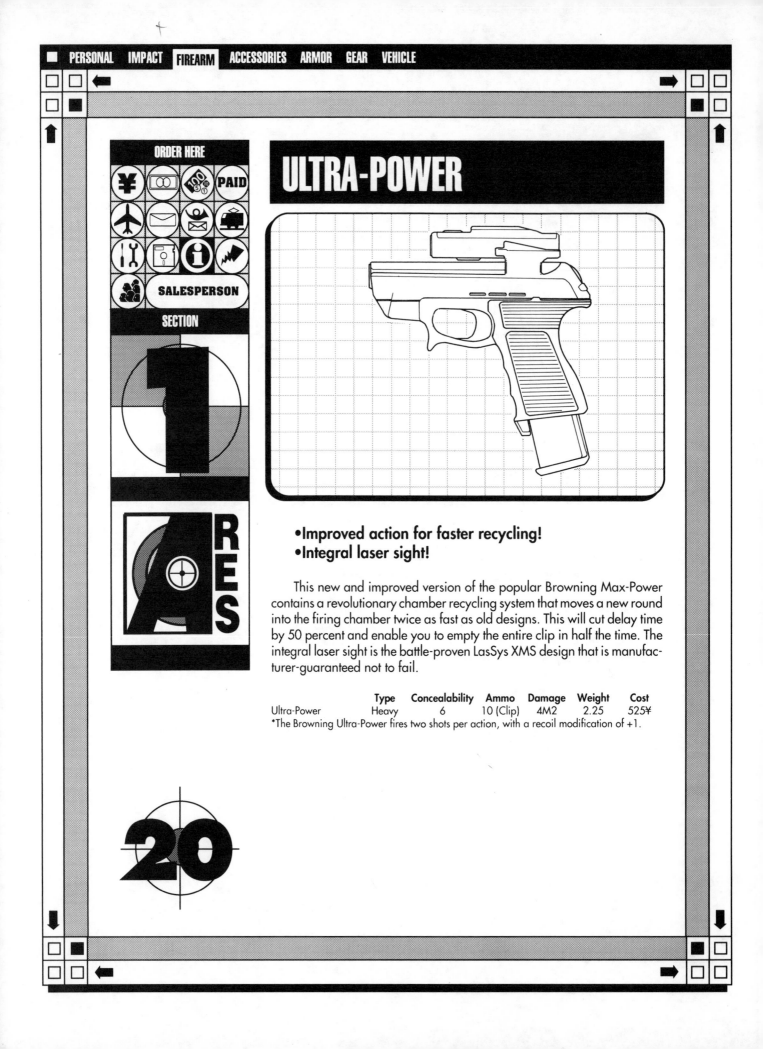

- •Improved action for faster recycling!
- •Integral laser sight!

This new and improved version of the popular Browning Max-Power contains a revolutionary chamber recycling system that moves a new round into the firing chamber twice as fast as old designs. This will cut delay time by 50 percent and enable you to empty the entire clip in half the time. The integral laser sight is the battle-proven LasSys XMS design that is manufacturer-guaranteed not to fail.

	Type	Concealability	Ammo	Damage	Weight	Cost
Ultra-Power	Heavy	6	10 (Clip)	4M2	2.25	525¥

*The Browning Ultra-Power fires two shots per action, with a recoil modification of +1.

20

SCORPION MACHINE PISTOL

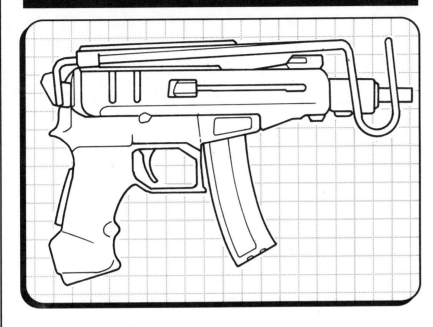

- •Combines light weight with full-auto capability!
- •Comes with integral folding stock!

This design by Ceska combines a submachine gun's rate-of-fire with the weight and concealability of a light service pistol. It comes equipped with an integral folding stock* for added recoil-reduction and it can carry all conventional pistol accessories. The optional extended-shot clip is also sure to please. Don't leave home without it!

	Type	Concealability	Ammo	Damage	Weight	Cost
Black Scorpion	Light	6	25 (Clip)	3M2	2.75	750¥
Black Scorpion	Light	5	35 (Clip)	3M2	3.0	850¥

*The Folding Shoulder Stock gives 1 point of Recoil Reduction.

ORDER HERE

PAID

SALESPERSON

SECTION

1

A R E S

CESKA vz/120

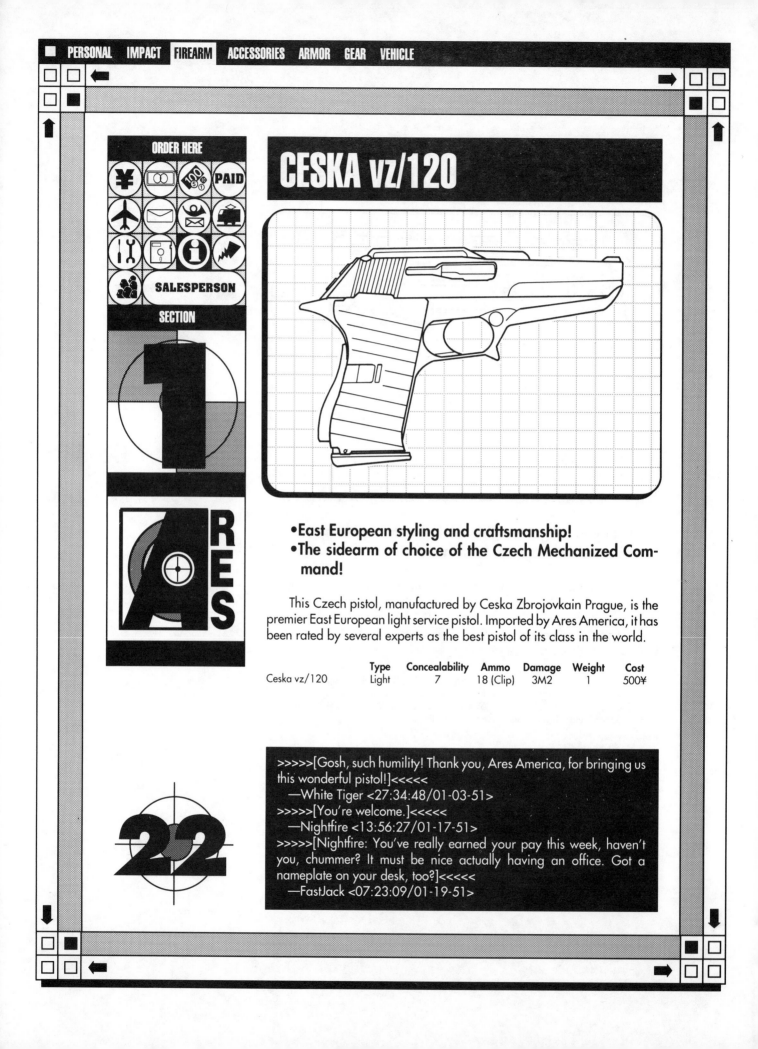

- **East European styling and craftsmanship!**
- **The sidearm of choice of the Czech Mechanized Command!**

This Czech pistol, manufactured by Ceska Zbrojovkain Prague, is the premier East European light service pistol. Imported by Ares America, it has been rated by several experts as the best pistol of its class in the world.

	Type	Concealability	Ammo	Damage	Weight	Cost
Ceska vz/120	Light	7	18 (Clip)	3M2	1	500¥

22

>>>>>[Gosh, such humility! Thank you, Ares America, for bringing us this wonderful pistol!]<<<<<
   —White Tiger <27:34:48/01-03-51>
>>>>>[You're welcome.]<<<<<
   —Nightfire <13:56:27/01-17-51>
>>>>>[Nightfire: You've really earned your pay this week, haven't you, chummer? It must be nice actually having an office. Got a nameplate on your desk, too?]<<<<<
   —FastJack <07:23:09/01-19-51>

MANHUNTER

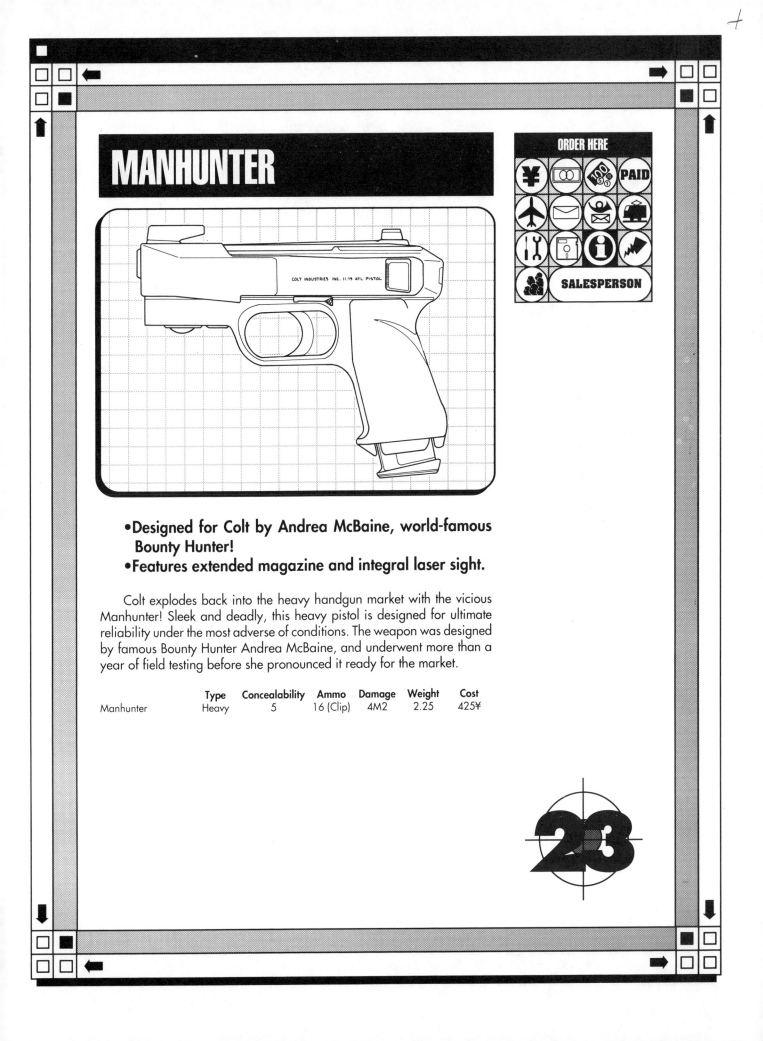

- **Designed for Colt by Andrea McBaine, world-famous Bounty Hunter!**
- **Features extended magazine and integral laser sight.**

Colt explodes back into the heavy handgun market with the vicious Manhunter! Sleek and deadly, this heavy pistol is designed for ultimate reliability under the most adverse of conditions. The weapon was designed by famous Bounty Hunter Andrea McBaine, and underwent more than a year of field testing before she pronounced it ready for the market.

	Type	Concealability	Ammo	Damage	Weight	Cost
Manhunter	Heavy	5	16 (Clip)	4M2	2.25	425¥

23

ORDER HERE

PAID

SALESPERSON

SECTION

1

ARES

LD-120

SECO INDUSTRIES LD-120 SLP-C

•**Precision craftsmanship from an Israeli design!**
•**Comes with integral mini-laser!**

Count on Seco to take the fantastic, but decades old, Israeli LD-100 design and rework it for modern times. Not only does it fire today's caseless high-compression rounds, but it also mounts an integral mini-laser for faster targeting! The sturdy flat-black macroplastic casing gives it that lethal look in such demand.

	Type	Concealability	Ammo	Damage	Weight	Cost
Seco LD-120	Light	5	12 (Clip)	3M2	1	400¥

24

>>>>>[Careful about this one, jokers. I found out the hard way that the "mini-laser" is good out to only about 20 meters. Can't really handle smoke, either.]<<<<<
—Findler-Man <22:31:03/12-17-50>
>>>>>[Truthfully? The one I own works fine out to a good 40–45 meters. Perhaps you have a damaged focusing system?]<<<<<
—Winger <09:47:54/12-23-50>

SELF-DEFENDER

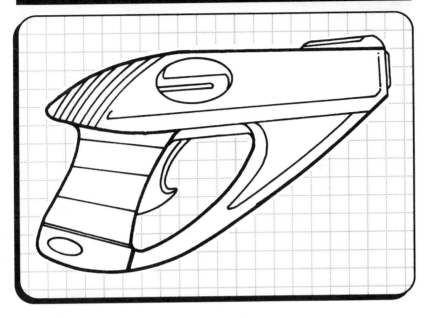

- •Lightweight, sleek design!
- •Perfect for concealment or undercover work!

The Tiffani Self-Defender, manufactured by Fichetti Firearms, answers the need of those who wanted a little more styling in their self-defense firearms. Small and easily concealable, it combines deadliness with a lethal fashion sense.

	Type	Concealability	Ammo	Damage	Weight	Cost
Tiffani Defender	Hold-out	8	4 (Clip)	3L1	.5	450¥

1

ARES

CMDT COMBAT GUN

- **•Rated best new weapon at Desert Wars 7!**
- **•The combat shotgun of militaries worldwide!**

Maybe the best combat shotgun on the market today. The Mossberg CMDT Combat Gun is a proven winner in every climate, in nearly every situation. Comes with integral laser sight, and the model SM variant has an internal smartgun link.

	Type	Concealability	Ammo	Damage	Weight	Cost
Mossberg CMDT	Shotgun	2	8 (Clip)	5M3	4.25	1,400¥
Mossberg CMDT/SM	Shotgun	2	8 (Clip)	5M3	4.5	1,900¥

26

>>>>>[Desert Wars. Now there's a concept. Let's get all the corporations to field small armies and blow the drek out each other in a nuclear-blasted wasteland. Guaranteed ratings grabber.]<<<<<
—Stinger-Six <08:23:45/12-09-50>

100 SPORT RIFLE

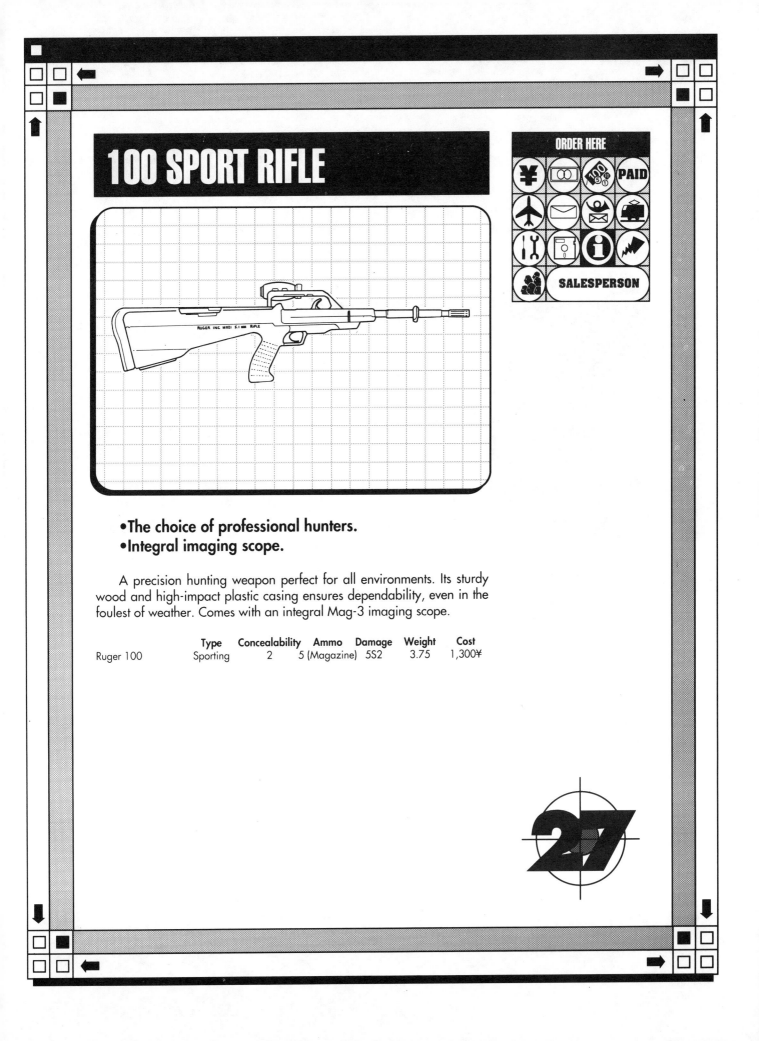

- •The choice of professional hunters.
- •Integral imaging scope.

A precision hunting weapon perfect for all environments. Its sturdy wood and high-impact plastic casing ensures dependability, even in the foulest of weather. Comes with an integral Mag-3 imaging scope.

	Type	Concealability	Ammo	Damage	Weight	Cost
Ruger 100	Sporting	2	5 (Magazine)	5S2	3.75	1,300¥

MA 2100 SNIPING RIFLE

- **The sniping rifle of the Confederated American States!**
- **Integral smartgun link!**

This weapon is the sniping rifle that just won the rigorous CAS Army sniper rifle competition! Designed to military specifications, the Walther is reliable and free of the design instabilities common to other weapons of the type. The professional's choice!

	Type	Concealability	Ammo	Damage	Weight	Cost
Walther MA 2100	Sniper	NA	8 (Magazine)	6S2	4.5	6,500¥

BERETTA MODEL 70

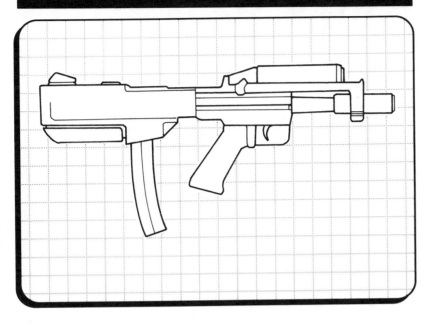

- •Integral laser sight and sound suppressor!
- •Largest ammo capacity of any SMG on the market!

The Beretta Model 70 holds the distinction, at 35 rounds, of having the greatest ammo capacity available in an SMG today! Combine that with an integral laser sight and sound suppressor, and you've got a weapon to arm the savage beast!

	Type	Concealability	Ammo	Damage	Weight	Cost
Beretta Model 70	SMG	3	35 (Clip)	4M3	3.75	900¥

>>>>>[A friend of mine has the Model 70. He says it's so quiet that all you can hear is the metal-on-metal sound of the bolt action. Pretty wiz...]<<<<<
—Lord Bunny <22:10:12/11-23-50>

ORDER HERE

¥ 💵 100% PAID

✈ ✉ 📫 🚋

🔧 💾 ⓘ ⚡

🞙 SALESPERSON

SECTION

1

ARES

MP-5 TX

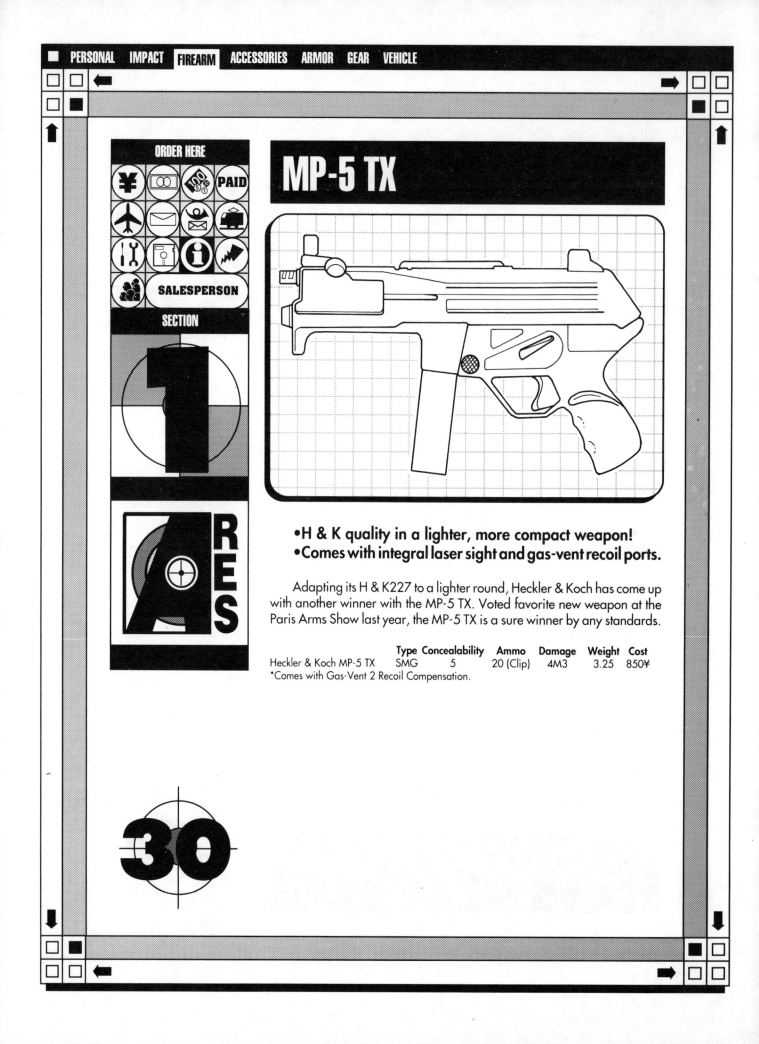

- •H & K quality in a lighter, more compact weapon!
- •Comes with integral laser sight and gas-vent recoil ports.

    Adapting its H & K227 to a lighter round, Heckler & Koch has come up with another winner with the MP-5 TX. Voted favorite new weapon at the Paris Arms Show last year, the MP-5 TX is a sure winner by any standards.

	Type	Concealability	Ammo	Damage	Weight	Cost
Heckler & Koch MP-5 TX	SMG	5	20 (Clip)	4M3	3.25	850¥

*Comes with Gas-Vent 2 Recoil Compensation.

30

INGRAM SMARTGUN

ORDER HERE

PAID

SALESPERSON

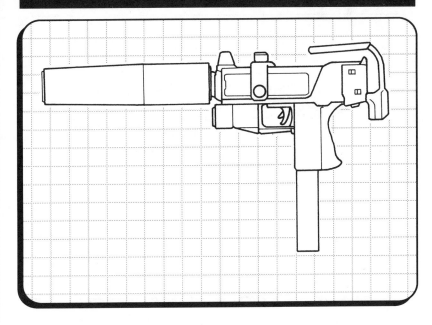

- Nicknamed "The Street Samurai's Sidekick"!
- Equipped with integral smartgun link and recoil suppression!
- Folding shoulder stock!

The May issue of *Street-Fighting Man* listed the Ingram Smartgun (Model 20t) as its readers' SMG of choice. One look and you'll see why more smart boys and girls carry the Ingram. Don't make the same mistake your enemy did. Carry the Model 20t.

	Type	Concealability	Ammo	Damage	Weight	Cost
Ingram Smartgun	SMG	5	32 (Clip)	5M3	3.0	950¥

>>>>>["The Street Samurai Sidekick"??? Just who do they think they're selling to? If only 'real' Street Samurai bought them, they'd barely sell any at all.]<<<<<
 —Findler-Man <06:34:04/12-19-50>
>>>>>[Yes, but remember there are a lot of street punks who like to think that they're 'real Street Samurai'. They buy guns too.]<<<<<
 —FastJack <19:03:27/12-20-50>

31

TMP SUBMACHINE GUN

- Sandler breaks the price barrier!
- Integral laser sight and folding stock!

The Sandler Corporation stunned the market earlier this year with the introduction of this high-quality, low-cost submachine gun. Displaying craftsmanship normally only expected from the best weaponsmiths, the Sandler TMP is certified popular with the professional who demands the best.

	Type	Concealability	Ammo	Damage	Weight	Cost
Sandler TMP	SMG	4	20 (Clip)	4M3	3.25	500¥

*Folding Stock provides 1 point of Recoil Reduction.

32

>>>>>[A former associate of mine had a TMP disintegrate in his hands at the most inopportune moment. Use with caution, or at least make sure the screws are tight.]<<<<<
—Hermes <09:32:19/12-17-50>

MODEL 100 SMG

ORDER HERE

SALESPERSON

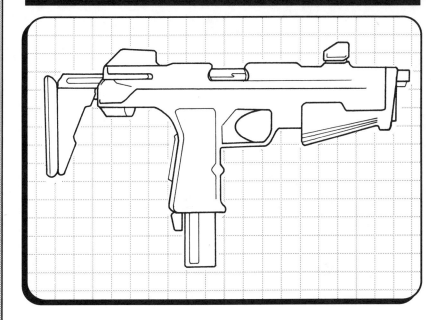

- **•The Japanese Security Forces weapon of choice!**
- **•Comes with integral smartgun link!**

Manufactured by Shin Chou Kogyo, Tokyo, the SCK Model 100 is used by more Japanese Security Forces worldwide than any other submachine gun. Rumor tells that even the elite Red Samurai pack this weapon! When it's time to pick the best, choose the one the best picked!

	Type	Concealability	Ammo	Damage	Weight	Cost
SCK Model 100	SMG	4	30 (Clip)	5M3	4.5	1,000¥

ORDER HERE

PAID

SALESPERSON

SECTION

1

ARES

34

CLIPS AND MAGAZINES

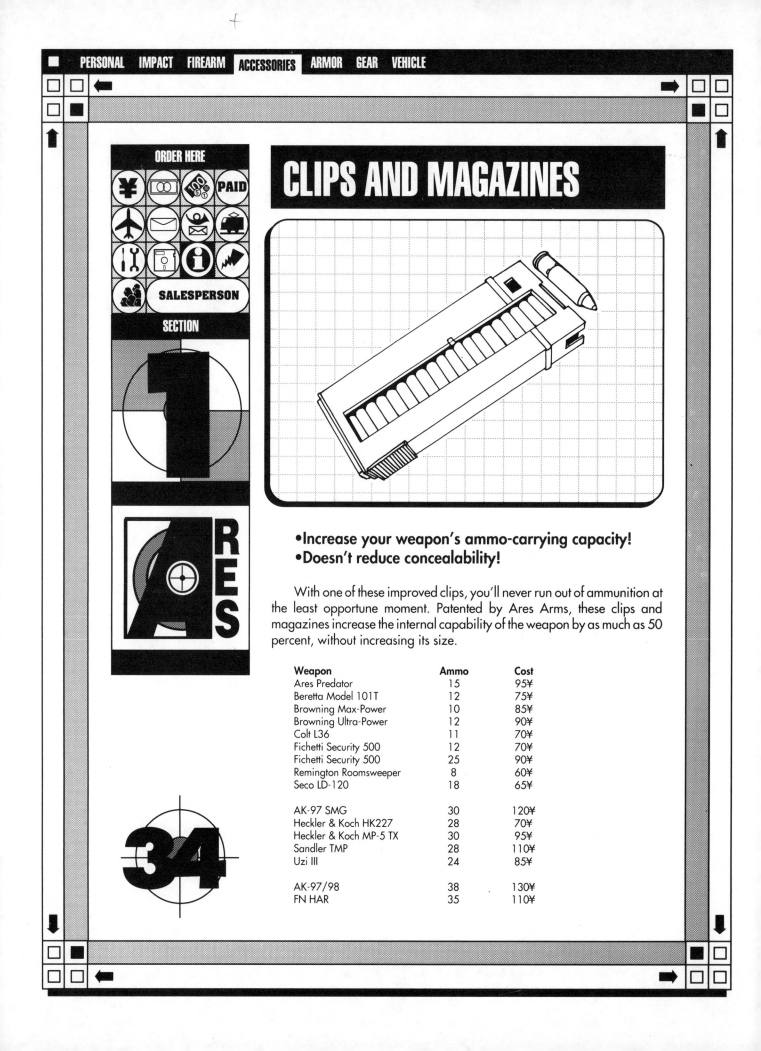

- •Increase your weapon's ammo-carrying capacity!
- •Doesn't reduce concealability!

With one of these improved clips, you'll never run out of ammunition at the least opportune moment. Patented by Ares Arms, these clips and magazines increase the internal capability of the weapon by as much as 50 percent, without increasing its size.

Weapon	Ammo	Cost
Ares Predator	15	95¥
Beretta Model 101T	12	75¥
Browning Max-Power	10	85¥
Browning Ultra-Power	12	90¥
Colt L36	11	70¥
Fichetti Security 500	12	70¥
Fichetti Security 500	25	90¥
Remington Roomsweeper	8	60¥
Seco LD-120	18	65¥
AK-97 SMG	30	120¥
Heckler & Koch HK227	28	70¥
Heckler & Koch MP-5 TX	30	95¥
Sandler TMP	28	110¥
Uzi III	24	85¥
AK-97/98	38	130¥
FN HAR	35	110¥

FIREPOWER™ AMMO

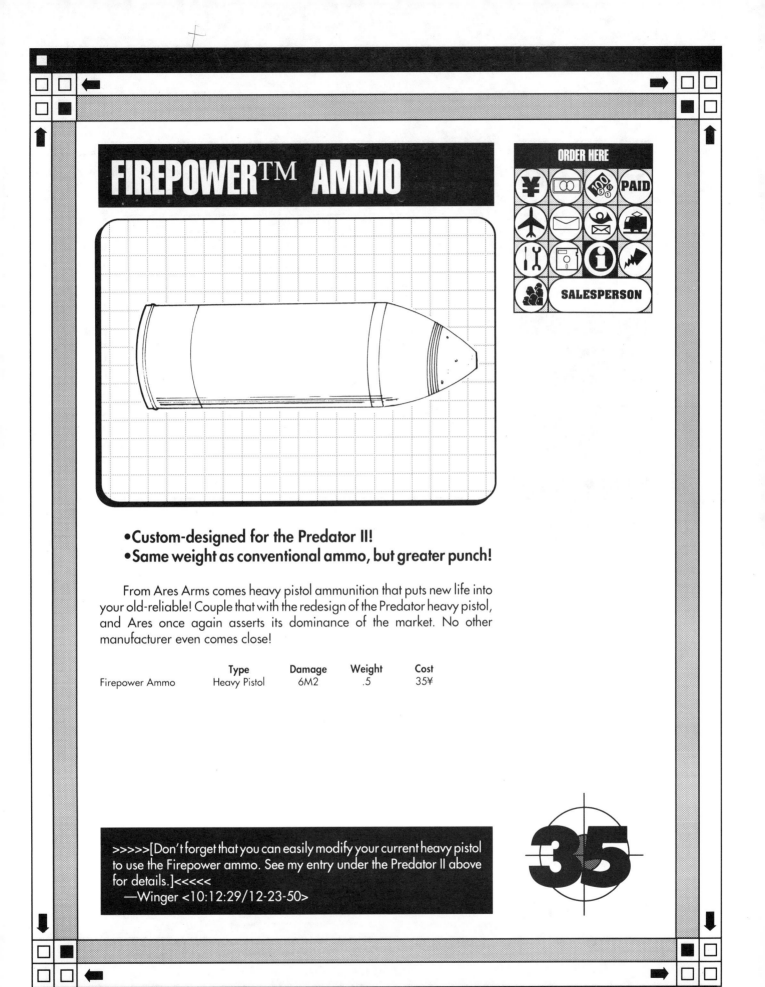

- •**Custom-designed for the Predator II!**
- •**Same weight as conventional ammo, but greater punch!**

From Ares Arms comes heavy pistol ammunition that puts new life into your old-reliable! Couple that with the redesign of the Predator heavy pistol, and Ares once again asserts its dominance of the market. No other manufacturer even comes close!

	Type	Damage	Weight	Cost
Firepower Ammo	Heavy Pistol	6M2	.5	35¥

>>>>>[Don't forget that you can easily modify your current heavy pistol to use the Firepower ammo. See my entry under the Predator II above for details.]<<<<<
—Winger <10:12:29/12-23-50>

35

ORDER HERE

¥   ⬭   100   PAID

✈   ✉   ☺   🚋

🔧   💾   ⓘ   ⚡

👥   SALESPERSON

SECTION

1

A R E S

ULTRASOUND SIGHT

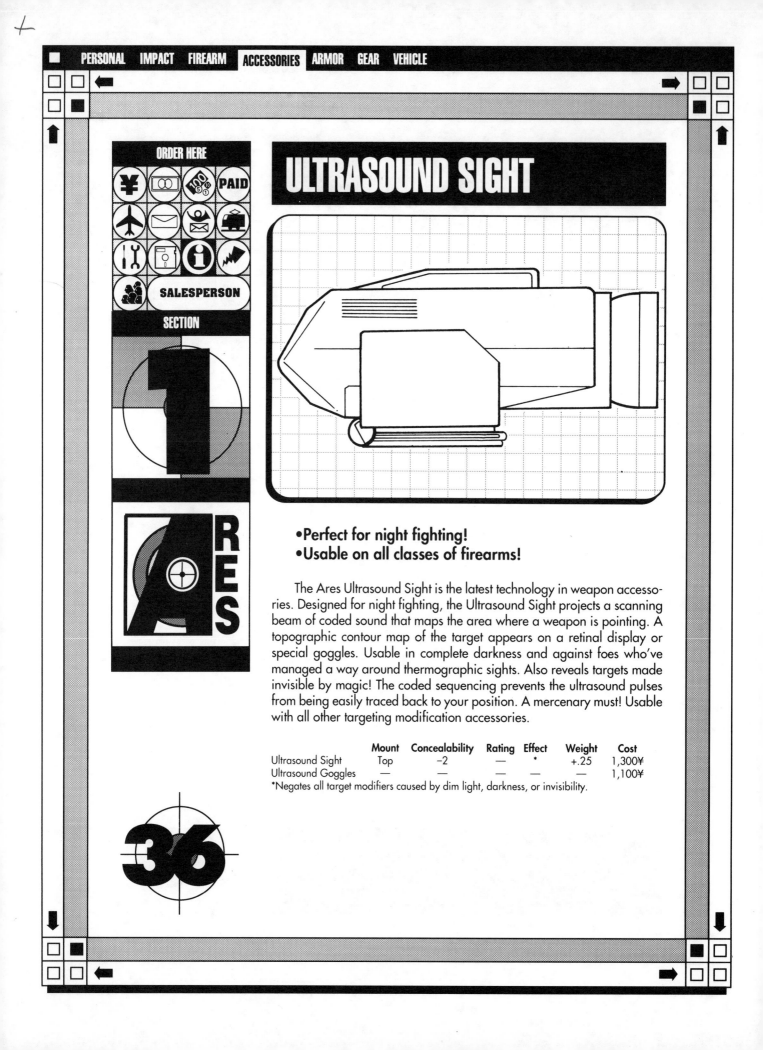

- •Perfect for night fighting!
- •Usable on all classes of firearms!

The Ares Ultrasound Sight is the latest technology in weapon accessories. Designed for night fighting, the Ultrasound Sight projects a scanning beam of coded sound that maps the area where a weapon is pointing. A topographic contour map of the target appears on a retinal display or special goggles. Usable in complete darkness and against foes who've managed a way around thermographic sights. Also reveals targets made invisible by magic! The coded sequencing prevents the ultrasound pulses from being easily traced back to your position. A mercenary must! Usable with all other targeting modification accessories.

	Mount	Concealability	Rating	Effect	Weight	Cost
Ultrasound Sight	Top	−2	—	*	+.25	1,300¥
Ultrasound Goggles	—	—	—	—	—	1,100¥

*Negates all target modifiers caused by dim light, darkness, or invisibility.

36

RANGEFINDER ACCESSORY

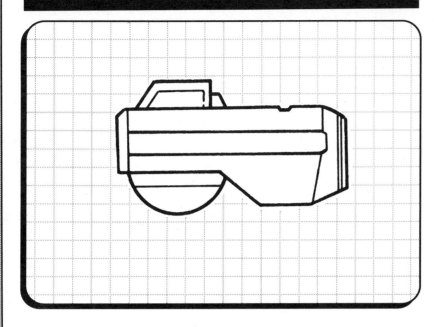

- **Ends distance-to-opponent guessing!**
- **Vital for use with rifle-mounted grenade launchers!**

The Ares Z2 Rangefinder is an underbarrel-mounted accessory that will feed range information through a smartgun link to a retinal display or smart-goggle display. In an instant, you can discover exactly how far away your opponent really is.

	Mount	Concealability	Weight	Cost
Rangefinder	Under	—	.1	150¥

>>>>>[Doesn't sound like it would be much help, eh? Just wait until you get to the Security catalog…]<<<<<
—FastJack <11:23:04/12-02-50>

GAS VENT

- •Steady that aim with the new Lyco System!
- •Usable with most firearm classes!

Lyco Systems of New Orleans has devised a new gas-vent recoil reduction system that is a great improvement over existing technology. Using a patented chamber system, the Lyco gas-vents are lighter, smaller, and more efficient than anything on the market today. Judge for yourself.

	Mount	Concealability	Rating	Weight	Cost
Imp.Gas-Vent 2	Barrel	—	2	.25	550¥
Imp.Gas-Vent 3	Barrel	−1	3	.5	800¥
Imp.Gas-Vent 4	Barrel	−2	4	.75	1,000¥

FOREARM GUARDS

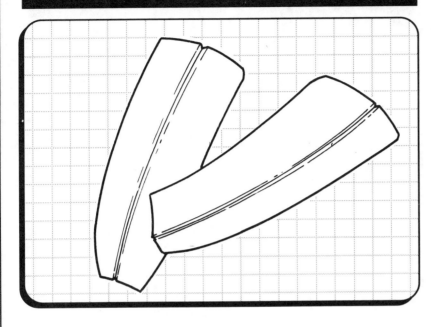

- **•The latest in defensive counterwear!**
- **•Here because you demanded it!**

After polling more than 1,000 hard-working people like you from around the country, Ares Arms has devised a new type of personal defense: forearm guards! Padded armorplast sections are form-fitted to each wearer, providing heavy impact protection across the back of each forearm. Designed specifically for parrying and forearm smashes! An instant street favorite!

	Concealability	Rating	Damage	Weight	Cost
Forearm Guards	12	+1*	(Str)M2	.2	250¥

*Gives the wearer an additional +1 of Impact Armor against unarmed and armed combat. Not good against ranged weapons of any kind.

>>>>>[Wonder how they polled the SINless?]<<<<<
—FastJack <11:28:09/12-02-50>

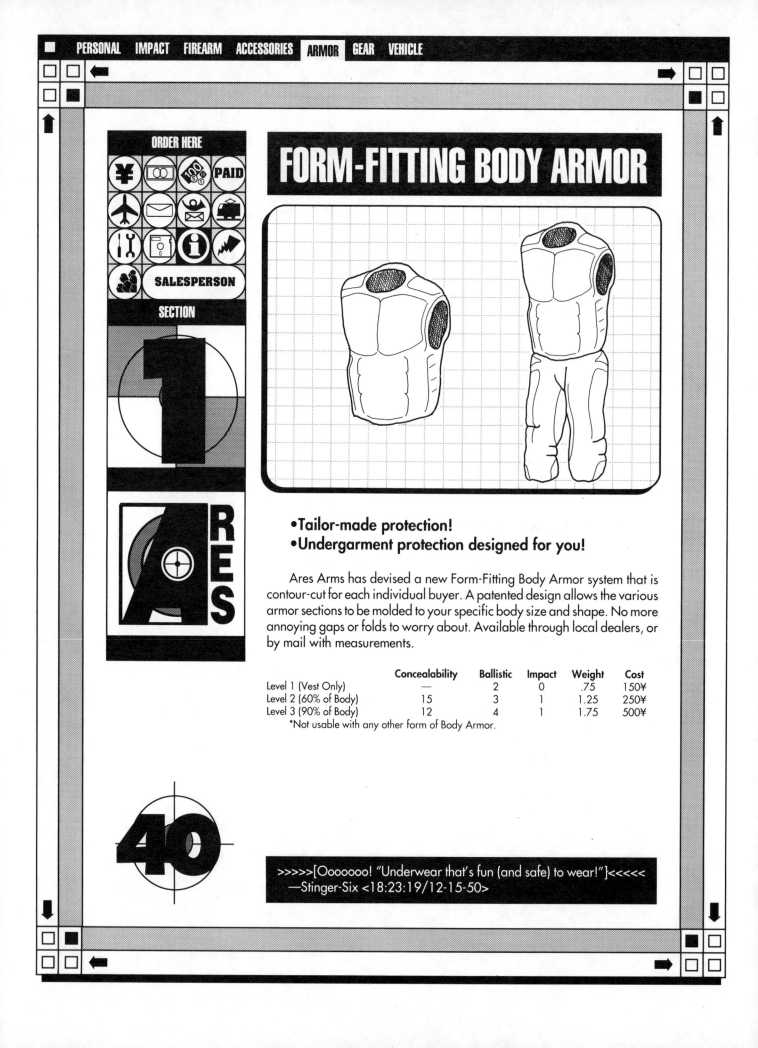

ORDER HERE

SECTION

SALESPERSON

FORM-FITTING BODY ARMOR

•Tailor-made protection!
•Undergarment protection designed for you!

Ares Arms has devised a new Form-Fitting Body Armor system that is contour-cut for each individual buyer. A patented design allows the various armor sections to be molded to your specific body size and shape. No more annoying gaps or folds to worry about. Available through local dealers, or by mail with measurements.

	Concealability	Ballistic	Impact	Weight	Cost
Level 1 (Vest Only)	—	2	0	.75	150¥
Level 2 (60% of Body)	15	3	1	1.25	250¥
Level 3 (90% of Body)	12	4	1	1.75	500¥

*Not usable with any other form of Body Armor.

>>>>>[Ooooooo! "Underwear that's fun (and safe) to wear!"]<<<<<
—Stinger-Six <18:23:19/12-15-50>

40

SECURETECH CLOTHING

ORDER HERE

SALESPERSON

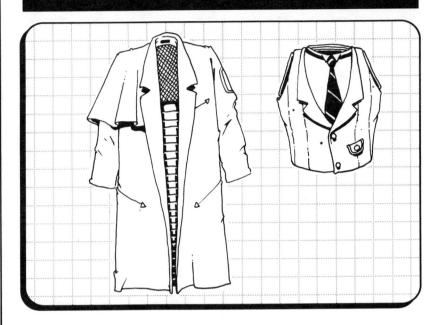

- **•The latest in protective body armor!**
- **•Many styles to choose from!**

Kelmar Technologies has cornered the market with their stylish line of protective clothing, and we are the first supplier in North America to provide you with the full line. Available in a full range of designer colors and styles. The technical specifications listed below are correct, unlike a certain other rival publication's. <Shadow Gear, Summer 2050 :: FJ>

	Concealability	Ballistic	Impact	Weight	Cost
Secure Clothing	12	3	0	1.5	450¥
Secure Jacket	9	5	3	3	850¥
Secure Vest	15	2	1	.75	175¥
Secure Ultra-Vest	14	3	2	2.5	350¥
Secure Long Coat	10	4	2	2.0	650¥

The Lined Coat adds 50 percent to the concealability rating of any weapon with a rating of 4 or higher.

ORDER HERE

SALESPERSON

SECTION

1

A R E S

STEALTH GRAPPLE LINE

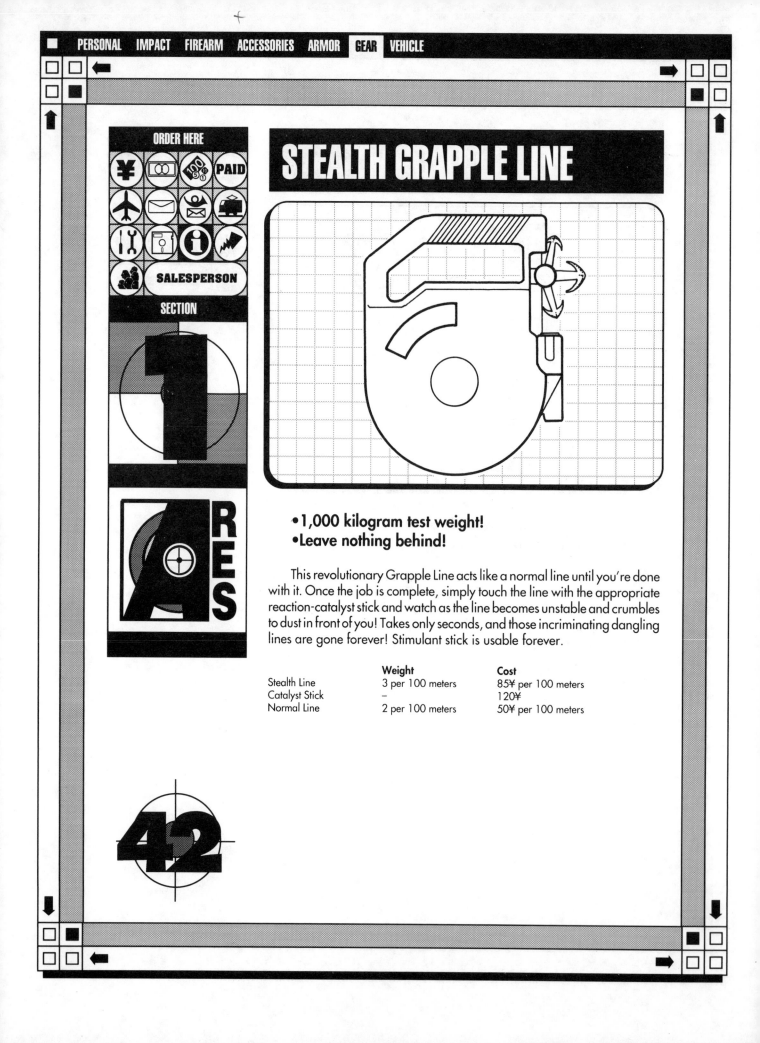

- •1,000 kilogram test weight!
- •Leave nothing behind!

This revolutionary Grapple Line acts like a normal line until you're done with it. Once the job is complete, simply touch the line with the appropriate reaction-catalyst stick and watch as the line becomes unstable and crumbles to dust in front of you! Takes only seconds, and those incriminating dangling lines are gone forever! Stimulant stick is usable forever.

	Weight	Cost
Stealth Line	3 per 100 meters	85¥ per 100 meters
Catalyst Stick	–	120¥
Normal Line	2 per 100 meters	50¥ per 100 meters

42

GRAPPLE GUN

ORDER HERE

SALESPERSON

- **Fires grapple hooks over 300 meters!**
- **Quiet and safe!**

The Conner Grapple Gun is the latest in grapple-propellant systems and is guaranteed to shoot the patented Wagner Grapple over 300 meters straight up! The grapple gun comes with its own internal spool, or external feed, for using the grapple line of your choice. Wagner rappelling gear fits snugly into the stock.

	Concealability	Weight	Cost
Grapple Gun	7	2.25	450¥
Rappelling Gear	—	5	250¥

*Use the Heavy Crossbow Range Table.

AFR-7 FLASH GRENADE

•Higher candle-power than ever before!

The AFR-7 is the most powerful flash grenade on the market. Weighing the same as a conventional grenade, it produces a blinding flash of light effective to 30 meters. Guaranteed ignition and improved burn characteristics make the AFR-7 the flash grenade of choice.

	Concealability	Damage	Effect	Weight	Cost
Flash Grenade	6	4L3*	30m**	.25	40¥

*Grenade has a blast-zone of 1 meter, inflicting damage of 3L3 within that area.
**Flash is effective out to 30 meters. Base target modification for all those looking in direction of grenade is +6. Target modifier is reduced by 1 for every 5 meters distance from the point of ignition. Flare Compensation reduces the target modifier by 50 percent (round down).

FLASH-PAK

- •**Distract and blind your opposition!**
- •**Small, compact, reusable!**

Another recently released winner from Winter Systems of Manhattan. The size of a cigarette pack, this small device contains four quartz-halogen micro-flashes designed to fire in random sequence to create a series of searing flashes that disorient, distract, and possibly even blind anyone looking in their direction! Works even against cybereyes with flare compensation!

	Concealability	Rating	Weight	Cost
Flash-Pak*	12	+4	.2	250¥

*Use of a flash-pak gives opponents facing the flash-pak a +4 target modifier to all ranged attacks. Opponents with flare-compensation receive only a +2. Target modification is reduced by 1 for every 5 meters from the Flash-Pak. The Pak also negates effects of poor or no lighting for the duration of its use, but does impose its own +2 because of its stroboscopic nature.

>>>>>[Why do I read this and hear the words of a very old song…something about being blinded by the light, and then running in the night?]<<<<<
—Steel Lynx <13:55:35/12-20-50>

45

ORDER HERE

SALESPERSON

SECTION

1

MICRO FLARE

- **A penlight-sized flare launcher!**
- **Perfect for those sudden emergencies!**

Winter Systems of Manhattan has finally released one of its patented mini-system security devices to the general public, the Micro Flare. A little larger than a penlight, the Micro Flare packs a full-size warning/hazard flare. Capable of reaching altitudes in excess of 200 meters, the flare is available in white, red, or green. Reloadable, it makes the perfect emergency signalling device.

	Concealability	Rating	Weight	Cost
Micro Flare Launcher*	3	2	2	50¥
Flare	—	2	—	75¥

*If fired as a weapon, use the Bow Range Table, plus an additional +2 target modifier at all ranges beyond Short. The weapon will inflict 3M3 damage, and ignite flammables. The Rating indicates that the flare will negate a +2 target modifier due to low or poor light. The flare will illuminate an area equal to one square city block.

46

AURORA RACING BIKE

ORDER HERE

SALESPERSON

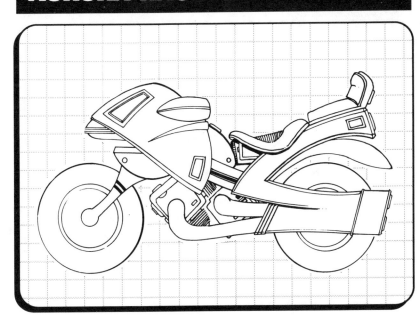

- **Low and sleek, the Aurora is the fastest bike on the streets!**
- **Maximum power and style!**

The Aurora, new from Suzuki Transport, is guaranteed to wipe the smile off the face of any cocky Yamaha Rapier jockey. Designed for speed, the Aurora features advanced ride-stabilization equipment for superb handling and control. Buy today and we'll throw in a custom paint job so those Rapiers will know exactly who blew them away.

	Handling	Speed	Body	Armor	Signature	Pilot	Cost
Suzuki Aurora	2	70/210	1	0	4	1	15,000¥

(The Aurora, like the Rapier, is unable to accept either a firmpoint or hardpoint. The Harley Scorpion is able to accept up to 2 firmpoints or 1 hardpoint. A firmpoint costs 10 percent of the vehicle cost and a hardpoint 30 percent.)

ORDER HERE

SALESPERSON

SECTION

1

A
R
E
S

VIKING HEAVY MOTORCYCLE

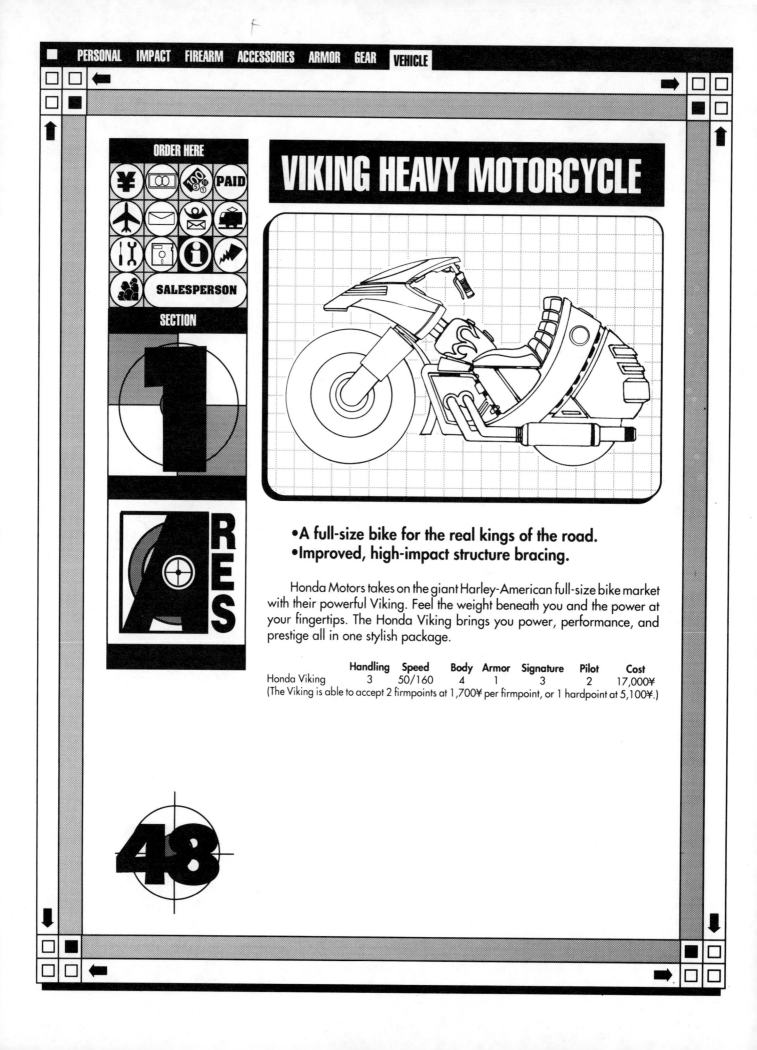

•A full-size bike for the real kings of the road.
•Improved, high-impact structure bracing.

Honda Motors takes on the giant Harley-American full-size bike market with their powerful Viking. Feel the weight beneath you and the power at your fingertips. The Honda Viking brings you power, performance, and prestige all in one stylish package.

	Handling	Speed	Body	Armor	Signature	Pilot	Cost
Honda Viking	3	50/160	4	1	3	2	17,000¥

(The Viking is able to accept 2 firmpoints at 1,700¥ per firmpoint, or 1 hardpoint at 5,100¥.)

48

ARES CATALOG WINTER 2050

1

ARES SECURITY

2

WIREMASTERS

3

ACCESSORIES

4

ARES SECURITY CATALOG 2050

You demand the best, and that's why you've chosen Ares America for over 25 years. Performance and reliability are what make Ares weapons and accessories the perfect choice for your security needs.

Within these pages, you will find the best security and law-enforcement equipment from manufacturers world-wide. Each item has been rigorously tested in the Ares laboratories and has met or exceeded our requirements for durability and dependability.

If you see it in these pages, you can count on it.

Contact your local Ares America sales representative, or call us directly at NA/UCAS-MW/BULLETS. We'll be expecting you.

—Nathaniel Naidich, Director of Sales, Ares America

Ares America is a division of Ares Arms, a wholly owned subsidiary of Ares Macrotechnology Incorporated, Detroit, Michigan, UCAS.

>>>>>[For those who don't know, the Ares America Security Catalog is difficult to obtain. When asked, the Ares sales and public relations departments will deny its existence. It's available only to licensed law enforcement, military, and security organizations with a valid, current credit rating. Don't ask me what they're trying to hide, but…feel free to post and comment as you like.]<<<<<
—FastJack <14:39:02/10-07-50>

>>>>>[One of you out there downloaded this file from the data net just after I posted it and attempted to sell it off to Ares' major competitor. You know who you are, and your deck is mine for the taking. Think about that the next time you're in some cold, dark corner of the Matrix.]<<<<<
—FastJack <23:43:43/10-07-50>

M22A2 ASSAULT RIFLE

ORDER HERE

SALESPERSON

SECTION

2

ARES

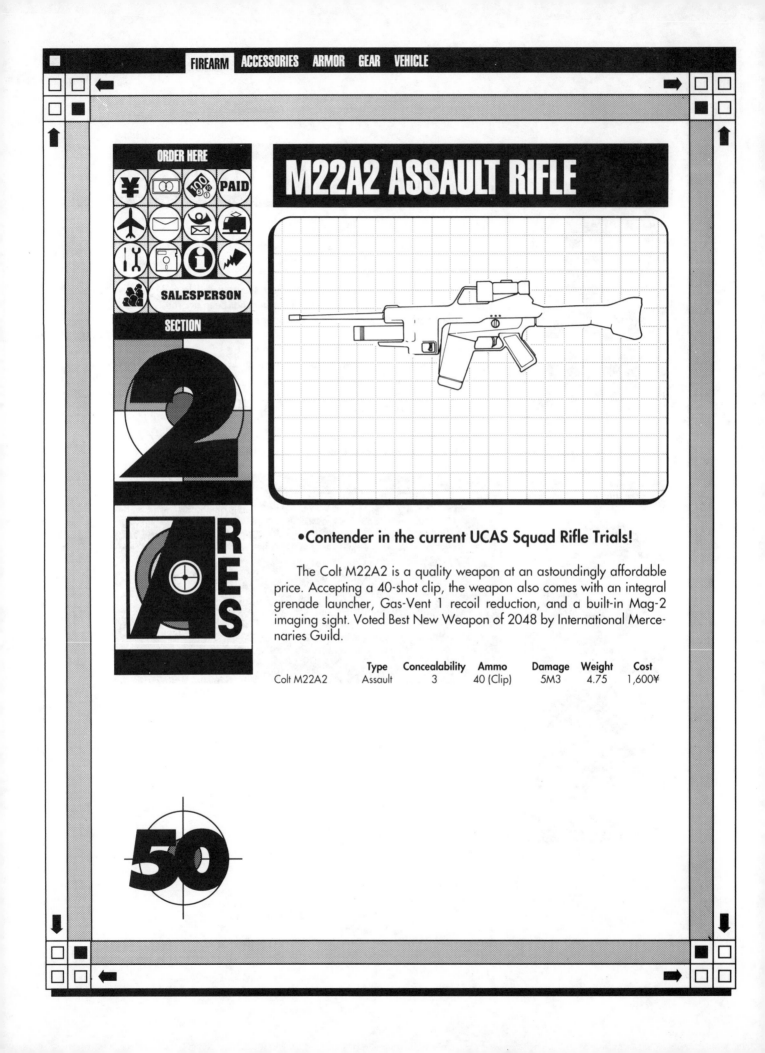

•Contender in the current UCAS Squad Rifle Trials!

The Colt M22A2 is a quality weapon at an astoundingly affordable price. Accepting a 40-shot clip, the weapon also comes with an integral grenade launcher, Gas-Vent 1 recoil reduction, and a built-in Mag-2 imaging sight. Voted Best New Weapon of 2048 by International Mercenaries Guild.

	Type	Concealability	Ammo	Damage	Weight	Cost
Colt M22A2	Assault	3	40 (Clip)	5M3	4.75	1,600¥

50

G12A3Z

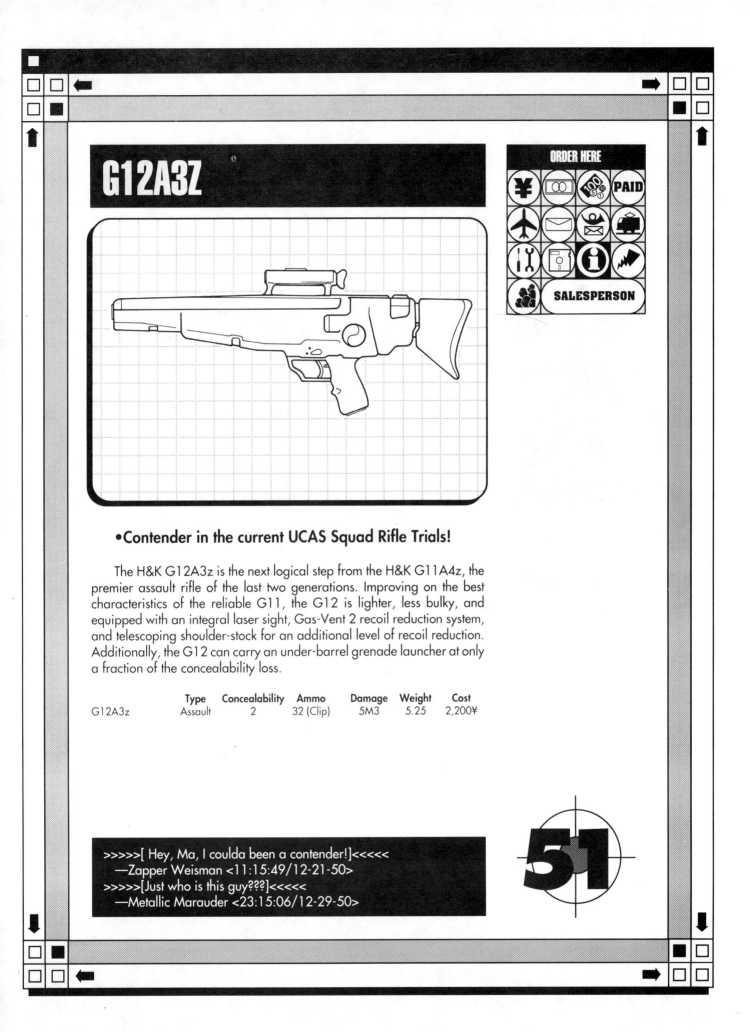

•Contender in the current UCAS Squad Rifle Trials!

The H&K G12A3z is the next logical step from the H&K G11A4z, the premier assault rifle of the last two generations. Improving on the best characteristics of the reliable G11, the G12 is lighter, less bulky, and equipped with an integral laser sight, Gas-Vent 2 recoil reduction system, and telescoping shoulder-stock for an additional level of recoil reduction. Additionally, the G12 can carry an under-barrel grenade launcher at only a fraction of the concealability loss.

	Type	Concealability	Ammo	Damage	Weight	Cost
G12A3z	Assault	2	32 (Clip)	5M3	5.25	2,200¥

>>>>>[Hey, Ma, I coulda been a contender!]<<<<<
   —Zapper Weisman <11:15:49/12-21-50>
>>>>>[Just who is this guy???]<<<<<
   —Metallic Marauder <23:15:06/12-29-50>

51

ORDER HERE

SALESPERSON

SECTION

2

RES

vz 88 V ASSAULT RIFLE

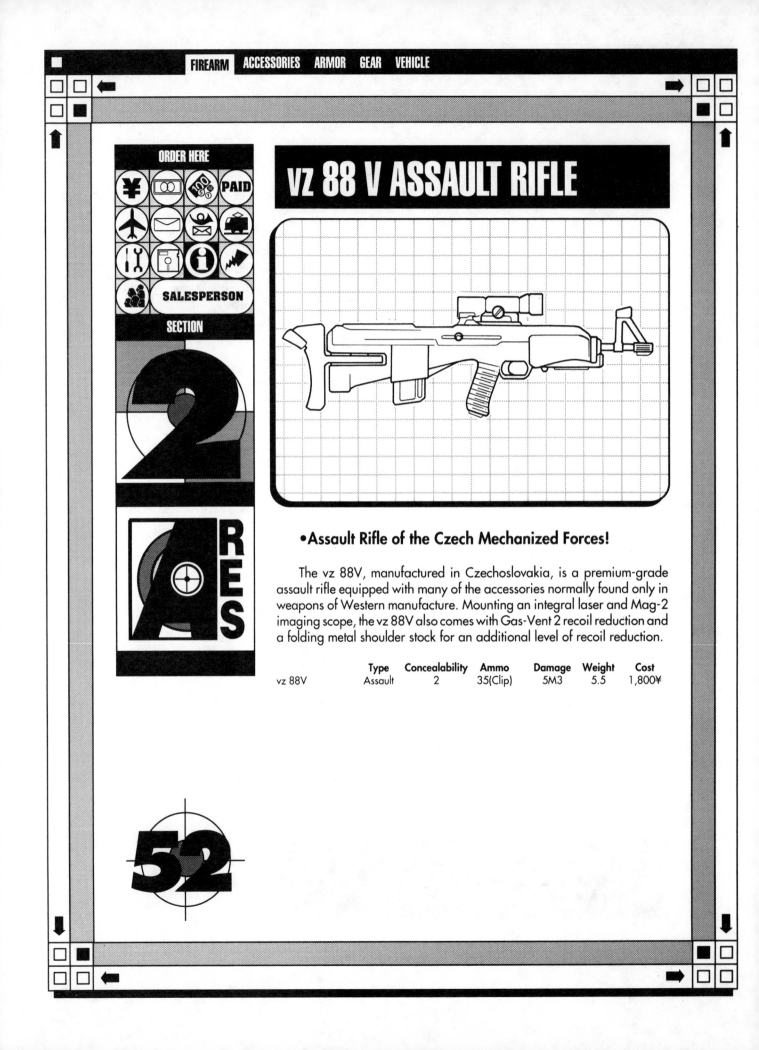

•Assault Rifle of the Czech Mechanized Forces!

The vz 88V, manufactured in Czechoslovakia, is a premium-grade assault rifle equipped with many of the accessories normally found only in weapons of Western manufacture. Mounting an integral laser and Mag-2 imaging scope, the vz 88V also comes with Gas-Vent 2 recoil reduction and a folding metal shoulder stock for an additional level of recoil reduction.

	Type	Concealability	Ammo	Damage	Weight	Cost
vz 88V	Assault	2	35(Clip)	5M3	5.5	1,800¥

AUG-CSL WEAPON SYSTEM

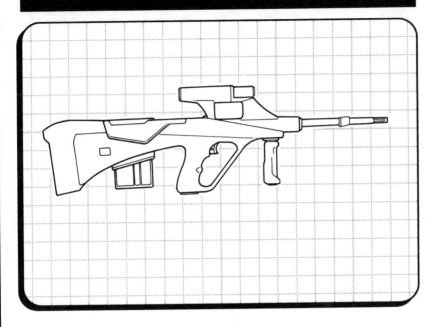

•The assault rifle of the Confederated American States!

The AUG-CSL is a multi-weapon, capable of being reassembled, variously, as a submachine gun, a carbine, an assault rifle, or a heavy-barreled automatic rifle for use as a light machine gun. Conversion takes just under one minute, and all the parts can fit into a large briefcase. All models have an integral laser sight in the carrying handle and can fit a smartgun adapter at no loss of concealability.

	Type	Concealability	Ammo	Damage	Weight	Cost
Steyr SMG	SMG	4	40 (Clip)	4M3	3.5	*
Carbine	Sporting	3	40 (Clip)	5M3	3.75	*
Assault Rifle	Assault	2	40 (Clip)	5M3	4	*
Light MG	Light MG	NA	40 (clip)	6M3	5.5	*

*The entire Steyr AUG-CSL package with all listed accessories costs 4,500¥. The weapon also comes with Gas-Vent 1 recoil reduction.

>>>>>[When this first came out, my buddy Wedge was in heaven. He rushed right out, scooped one up, and proceeded to play. Everything was great, and Wedge had even contacted Steyr about some design improvements. One day, he got a little confused and mounted the Light MG barrel with the carbine folding-stock, and, well, broke his shoulder. Steyr plans a color-code system for parts, and Wedge says he likes his new shoulder better anyway.]<<<<<
—FastJack <16:21:43/12-21-50>

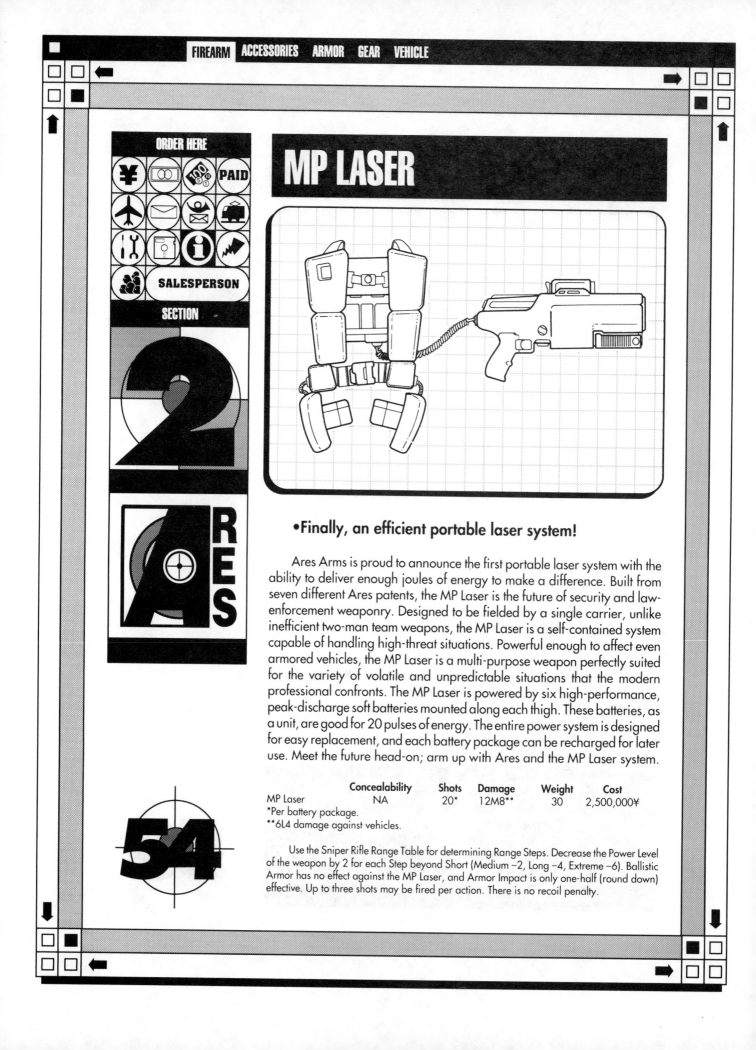

ORDER HERE

SALESPERSON

SECTION

2

MP LASER

•Finally, an efficient portable laser system!

Ares Arms is proud to announce the first portable laser system with the ability to deliver enough joules of energy to make a difference. Built from seven different Ares patents, the MP Laser is the future of security and law-enforcement weaponry. Designed to be fielded by a single carrier, unlike inefficient two-man team weapons, the MP Laser is a self-contained system capable of handling high-threat situations. Powerful enough to affect even armored vehicles, the MP Laser is a multi-purpose weapon perfectly suited for the variety of volatile and unpredictable situations that the modern professional confronts. The MP Laser is powered by six high-performance, peak-discharge soft batteries mounted along each thigh. These batteries, as a unit, are good for 20 pulses of energy. The entire power system is designed for easy replacement, and each battery package can be recharged for later use. Meet the future head-on; arm up with Ares and the MP Laser system.

	Concealability	Shots	Damage	Weight	Cost
MP Laser	NA	20*	12M8**	30	2,500,000¥

*Per battery package.
**6L4 damage against vehicles.

Use the Sniper Rifle Range Table for determining Range Steps. Decrease the Power Level of the weapon by 2 for each Step beyond Short (Medium –2, Long –4, Extreme –6). Ballistic Armor has no effect against the MP Laser, and Armor Impact is only one-half (round down) effective. Up to three shots may be fired per action. There is no recoil penalty.

54

MP LASER

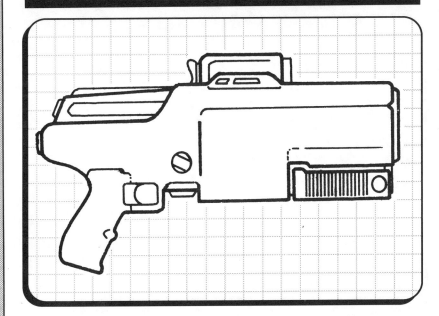

ORDER HERE

SALESPERSON

>>>>>[Can you believe this? This isn't a security or law-enforcement weapon; it's a military weapon. What the hell is it doing in a "security" catalog? Can we expect next year's catalog to include Seven-7 nerve gas, high-explosive, multiple high-velocity fragmenting claymore-style mines, and low-yield sub-tactical nukes? Let's get some chip-truth here, chummers. Has Ares lost it, or are they callously displaying the same blatant disregard for the "have-nots" as virtually every other security agency in existence? I have always considered Knight Errant to be one of the more respectable security/enforcement agencies, but after reading this document, I see I must have been horribly mistaken.]<<<<<
   —The Neon Samurai <01:17:24/12-09-50>

>>>>>[Hey, Neon, lighten up, will ya? Har-har!]<<<<<
   —Findler-Man <12:32:20/12-13-50>

>>>>>[I understand Winter Systems in Manhattan is working on a portable continuous laser that might reach production within a year. Allegedly, the prototype is able to maintain its beam for up to three minutes at a time and project up to 60 meters.]<<<<<
   —Hatchetman <21:45:03/12-17-50>

>>>>>[Don't believe anything, rather everything, you read.]<<<<<
   —Nightfire <04:05:48/12-18-50>

ORDER HERE

SALESPERSON

SECTION

2

ARES

ARES MP LMG

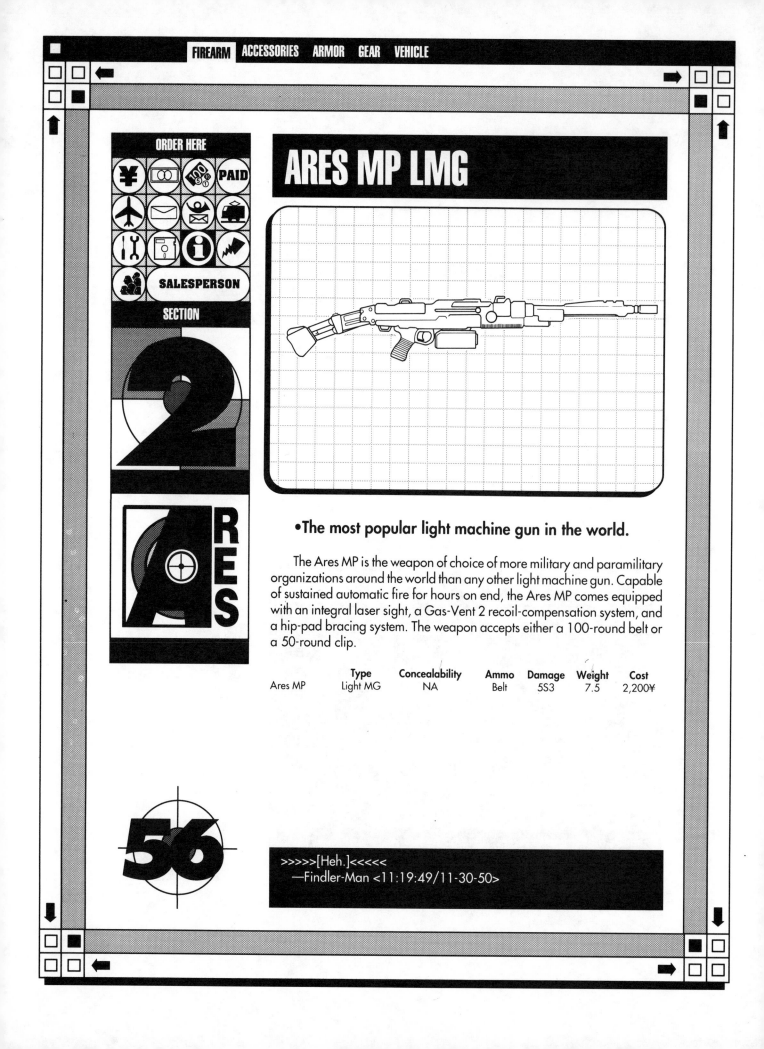

•The most popular light machine gun in the world.

The Ares MP is the weapon of choice of more military and paramilitary organizations around the world than any other light machine gun. Capable of sustained automatic fire for hours on end, the Ares MP comes equipped with an integral laser sight, a Gas-Vent 2 recoil-compensation system, and a hip-pad bracing system. The weapon accepts either a 100-round belt or a 50-round clip.

	Type	Concealability	Ammo	Damage	Weight	Cost
Ares MP	Light MG	NA	Belt	5S3	7.5	2,200¥

>>>>>[Heh.]<<<<<
—Findler-Man <11:19:49/11-30-50>

56

FN-MAG 5

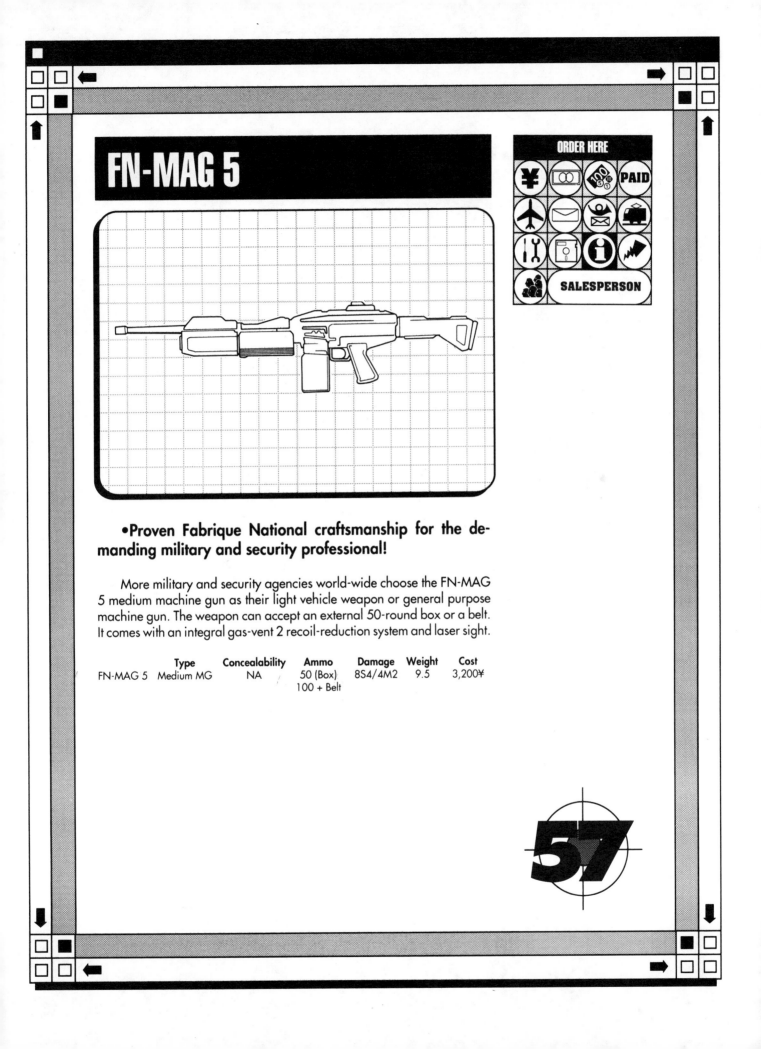

•**Proven Fabrique National craftsmanship for the demanding military and security professional!**

More military and security agencies world-wide choose the FN-MAG 5 medium machine gun as their light vehicle weapon or general purpose machine gun. The weapon can accept an external 50-round box or a belt. It comes with an integral gas-vent 2 recoil-reduction system and laser sight.

	Type	Concealability	Ammo	Damage	Weight	Cost
FN-MAG 5	Medium MG	NA	50 (Box) 100 + Belt	8S4/4M2	9.5	3,200¥

57

ORDER HERE

¥ | 💵 | 100 | PAID

SALESPERSON

SECTION

2

ARES

58

VINDICATOR MINIGUN

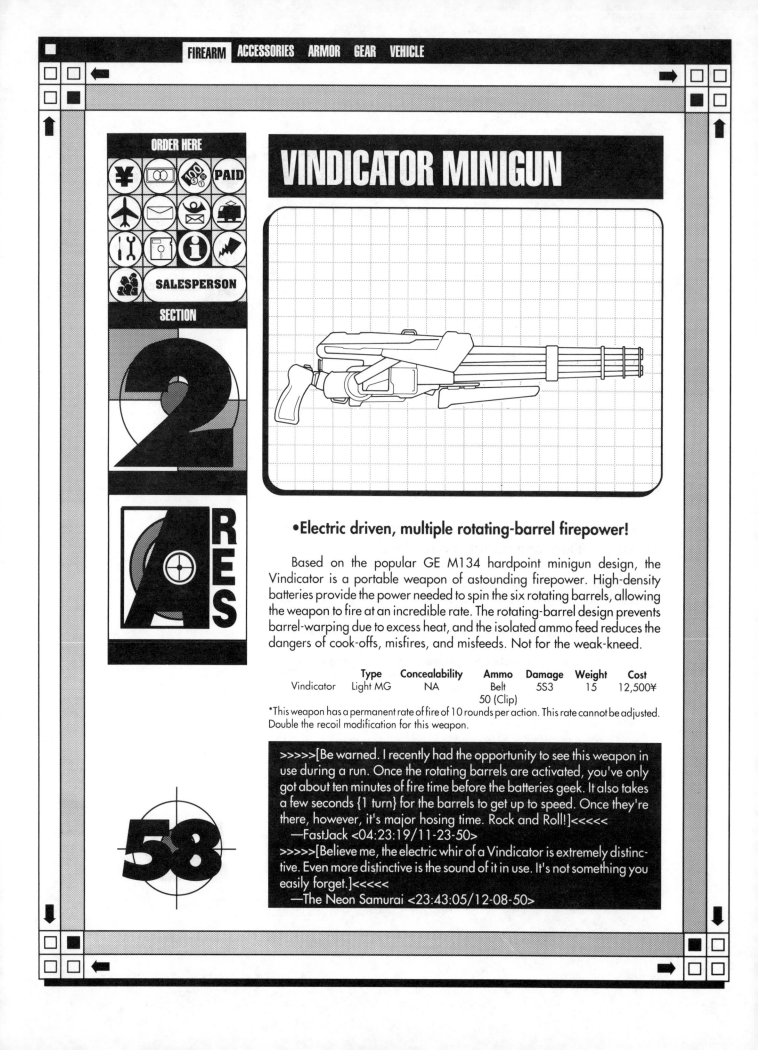

•Electric driven, multiple rotating-barrel firepower!

Based on the popular GE M134 hardpoint minigun design, the Vindicator is a portable weapon of astounding firepower. High-density batteries provide the power needed to spin the six rotating barrels, allowing the weapon to fire at an incredible rate. The rotating-barrel design prevents barrel-warping due to excess heat, and the isolated ammo feed reduces the dangers of cook-offs, misfires, and misfeeds. Not for the weak-kneed.

	Type	Concealability	Ammo	Damage	Weight	Cost
Vindicator	Light MG	NA	Belt 50 (Clip)	5S3	15	12,500¥

*This weapon has a permanent rate of fire of 10 rounds per action. This rate cannot be adjusted. Double the recoil modification for this weapon.

>>>>>[Be warned. I recently had the opportunity to see this weapon in use during a run. Once the rotating barrels are activated, you've only got about ten minutes of fire time before the batteries geek. It also takes a few seconds {1 turn} for the barrels to get up to speed. Once they're there, however, it's major hosing time. Rock and Roll!]<<<<<
—FastJack <04:23:19/11-23-50>
>>>>>[Believe me, the electric whir of a Vindicator is extremely distinctive. Even more distinctive is the sound of it in use. It's not something you easily forget.]<<<<<
—The Neon Samurai <23:43:05/12-08-50>

SURFACE-TO-AIR MISSILE

ORDER HERE

SALESPERSON

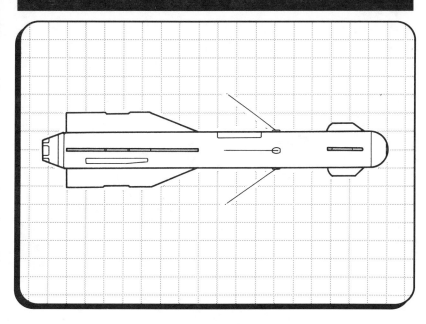

•Extended range for distant targets!

Designed for engaging long-distance aerial targets, this man-pack SAM is engineered for maximum velocity and anti-airframe impact. Compatible with any man-pack missile launcher, the SAM has a sophisticated on-board target acquisition and tracking seeker-head that has proven itself even against low, dodging targets.

	Intelligence	Damage	Weight	Cost
LR SAM	4	7D6/4M3	1.5	2,200¥

*Use the normal Missile Launcher Range Chart, but extend extreme range out to 5,000 meters.

>>>>>[I'll bet the Lone Star Wasp and Yellojacket flyers just love this joker.]<<<<<
    —Stinger-Six <18:22:23/01-12-51>

ORDER HERE

¥   PAID

SALESPERSON

SECTION

2

ARES

PANTHER CANNON

•Battle-proven maximum firepower!

The Panther Assault Cannon, designed and produced by Panther Industries, is your only choice for heavy assault weapon. Firing a stable superplast explosive warhead, the Panther has proven effective against both hard and soft targets. Comes with shoulder-strap and hip-bracing gear for stable fire.

	Type	Concealability	Ammo	Damage	Weight	Cost
Panther	Cannon	NA	22 (Clip) Belt	10D4/5S2	18	7,200¥

60

>>>>>[Grade A bang-bang!]<<<<<
—Hatchetman <23:17:54/12-17-50>

M107 GPHMG

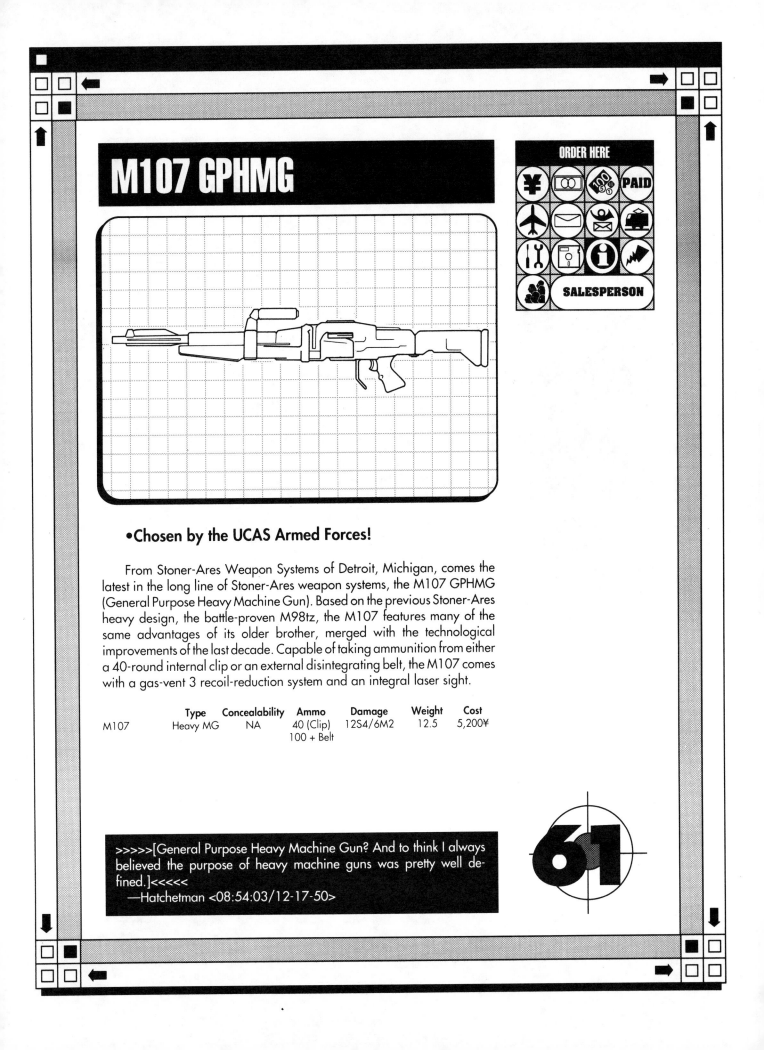

•Chosen by the UCAS Armed Forces!

From Stoner-Ares Weapon Systems of Detroit, Michigan, comes the latest in the long line of Stoner-Ares weapon systems, the M107 GPHMG (General Purpose Heavy Machine Gun). Based on the previous Stoner-Ares heavy design, the battle-proven M98tz, the M107 features many of the same advantages of its older brother, merged with the technological improvements of the last decade. Capable of taking ammunition from either a 40-round internal clip or an external disintegrating belt, the M107 comes with a gas-vent 3 recoil-reduction system and an integral laser sight.

	Type	Concealability	Ammo	Damage	Weight	Cost
M107	Heavy MG	NA	40 (Clip) 100 + Belt	12S4/6M2	12.5	5,200¥

>>>>>[General Purpose Heavy Machine Gun? And to think I always believed the purpose of heavy machine guns was pretty well defined.]<<<<<
—Hatchetman <08:54:03/12-17-50>

61

ORDER HERE

PAID

SALESPERSON

SECTION

2

ARES

NARCOJECT PISTOL & RIFLE

•The official Narcoject™ pistol and rifle!

The Narcoject™ pistol and rifle deliver patented Narcoject™ darts efficiently even under the most adverse combat conditions. The injection point of the dart can penetrate most armor reliably, ensuring target injection.

	Type	Concealability	Ammo	Damage	Weight	Cost
Narcoject Pistol	Light	7	5 (Clip)	**	1.5	600¥
Narcoject Rifle	Shotgun	4	10(Clip)	**	3.25	1,700¥
**Narcoject Round				**	.15	200¥

Usable only with the Narcoject Pistol or Rifle. (Weight per 10 rounds)
Delivers one dose of the Narcoject toxin (Shadowrun** rules, page 147). To penetrate a target's armor, firer must achieve more successes than the target's Impact Armor value. Target may use Dodge Pool successes to increase his armor value by 1 per success.

62

APDS AMMUNITION

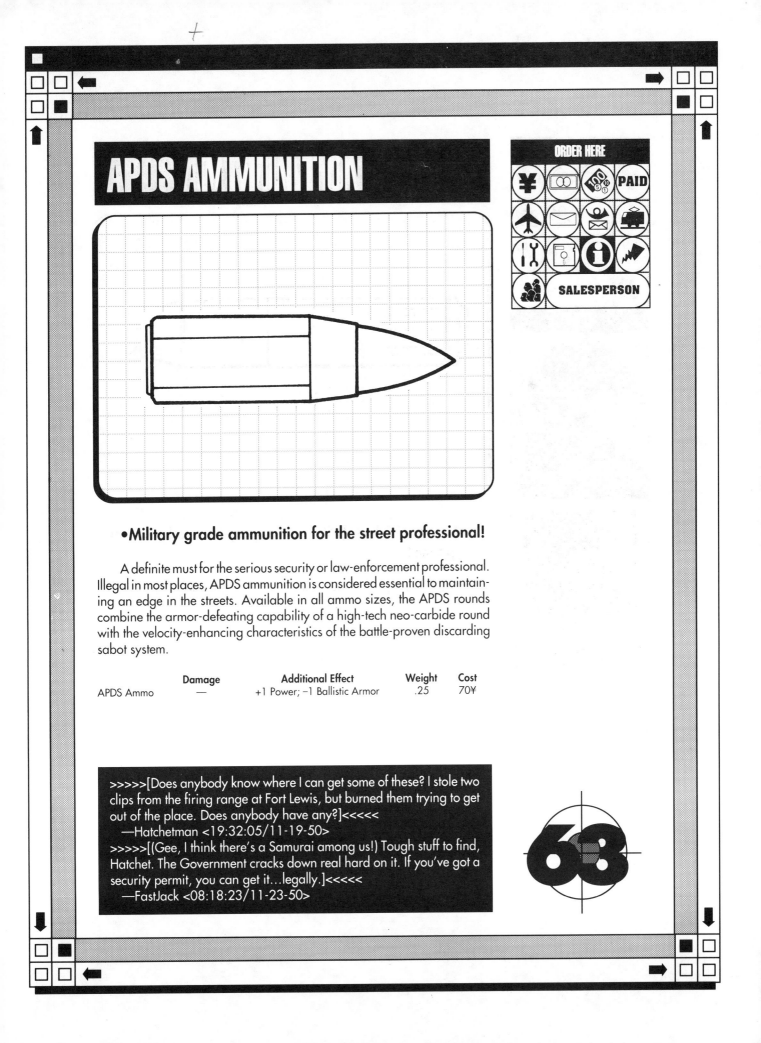

•Military grade ammunition for the street professional!

A definite must for the serious security or law-enforcement professional. Illegal in most places, APDS ammunition is considered essential to maintaining an edge in the streets. Available in all ammo sizes, the APDS rounds combine the armor-defeating capability of a high-tech neo-carbide round with the velocity-enhancing characteristics of the battle-proven discarding sabot system.

	Damage	Additional Effect	Weight	Cost
APDS Ammo	—	+1 Power; −1 Ballistic Armor	.25	70¥

>>>>>[Does anybody know where I can get some of these? I stole two clips from the firing range at Fort Lewis, but burned them trying to get out of the place. Does anybody have any?]<<<<<
 —Hatchetman <19:32:05/11-19-50>
>>>>>[(Gee, I think there's a Samurai among us!) Tough stuff to find, Hatchet. The Government cracks down real hard on it. If you've got a security permit, you can get it...legally.]<<<<<
 —FastJack <08:18:23/11-23-50>

63

ORDER HERE

SALESPERSON

SECTION

2

RES

CANNON AMMUNITION

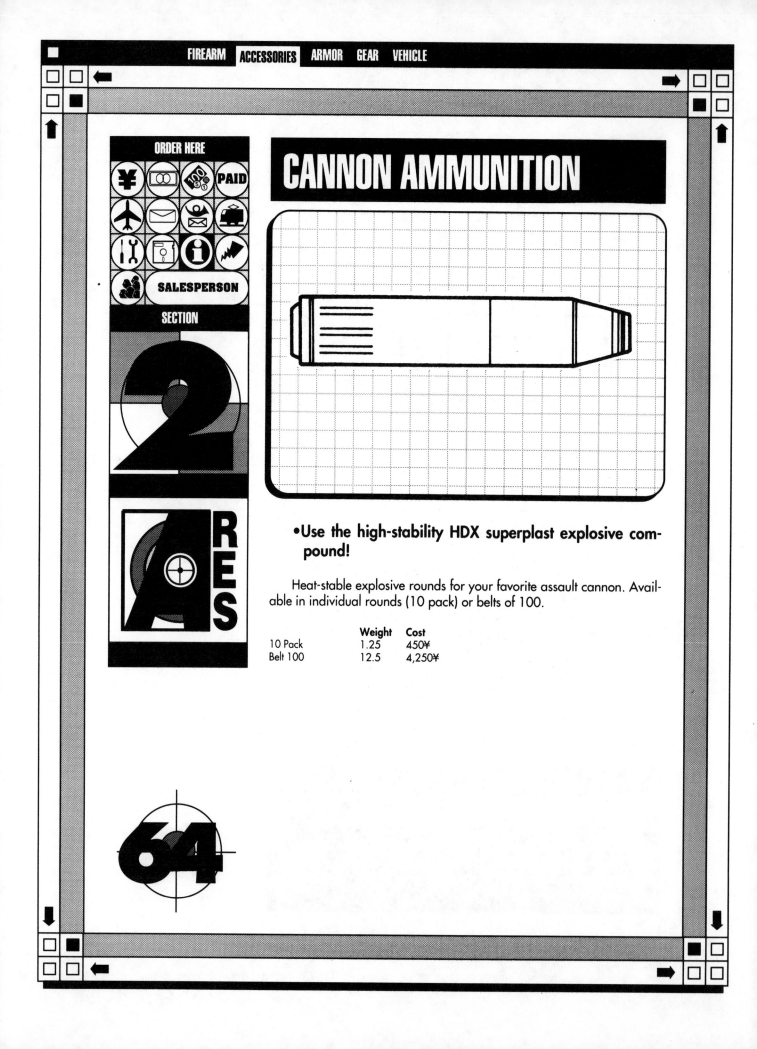

- **Use the high-stability HDX superplast explosive compound!**

Heat-stable explosive rounds for your favorite assault cannon. Available in individual rounds (10 pack) or belts of 100.

	Weight	Cost
10 Pack	1.25	450¥
Belt 100	12.5	4,250¥

64

BELTED AMMUNITION

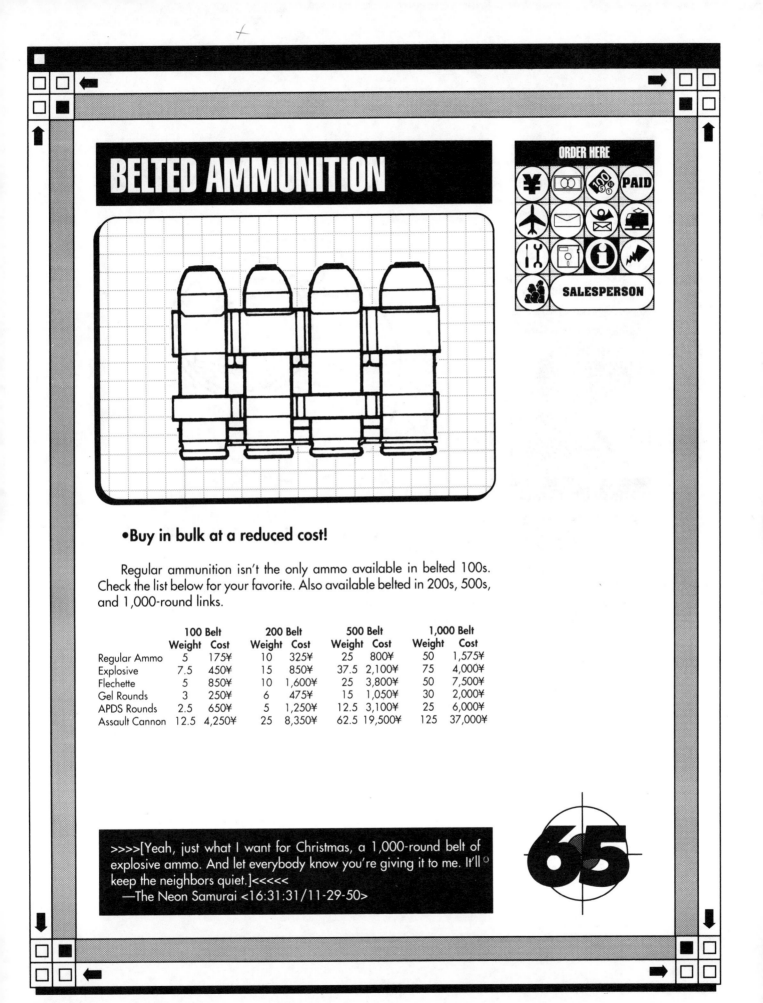

•Buy in bulk at a reduced cost!

Regular ammunition isn't the only ammo available in belted 100s. Check the list below for your favorite. Also available belted in 200s, 500s, and 1,000-round links.

	100 Belt		200 Belt		500 Belt		1,000 Belt	
	Weight	Cost	Weight	Cost	Weight	Cost	Weight	Cost
Regular Ammo	5	175¥	10	325¥	25	800¥	50	1,575¥
Explosive	7.5	450¥	15	850¥	37.5	2,100¥	75	4,000¥
Flechette	5	850¥	10	1,600¥	25	3,800¥	50	7,500¥
Gel Rounds	3	250¥	6	475¥	15	1,050¥	30	2,000¥
APDS Rounds	2.5	650¥	5	1,250¥	12.5	3,100¥	25	6,000¥
Assault Cannon	12.5	4,250¥	25	8,350¥	62.5	19,500¥	125	37,000¥

>>>>[Yeah, just what I want for Christmas, a 1,000-round belt of explosive ammo. And let everybody know you're giving it to me. It'll keep the neighbors quiet.]<<<<<
—The Neon Samurai <16:31:31/11-29-50>

65

ORDER HERE

SALESPERSON

SECTION

2

66

PERSONAL EXPLOSIVES

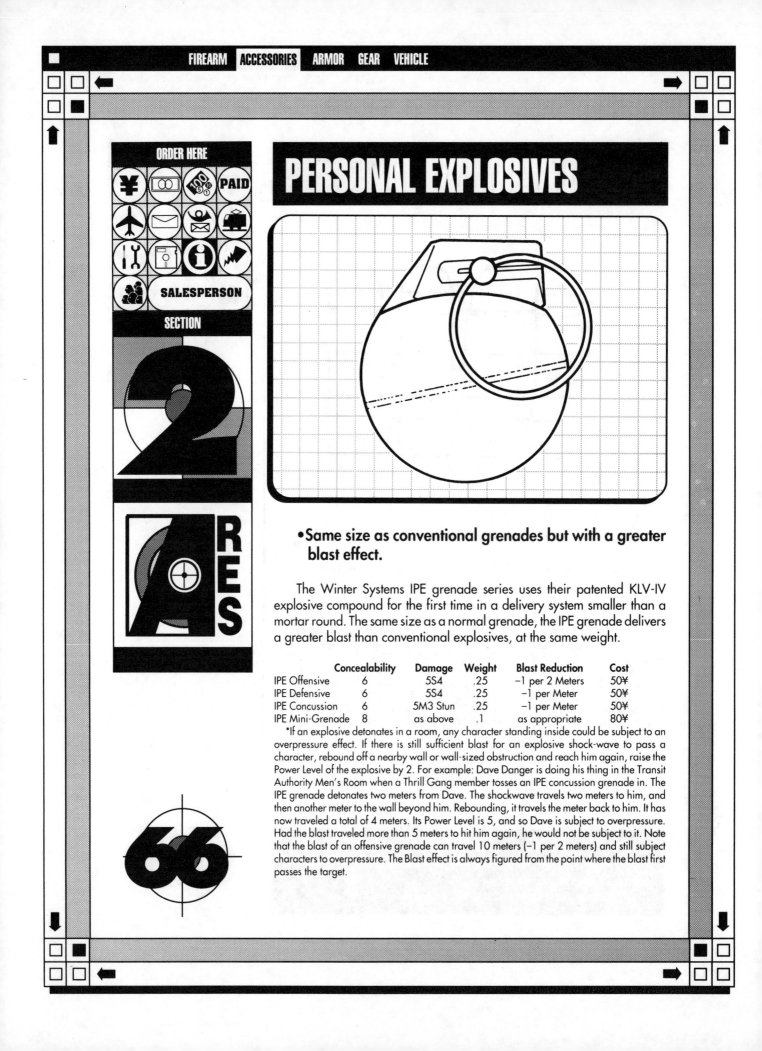

- **Same size as conventional grenades but with a greater blast effect.**

The Winter Systems IPE grenade series uses their patented KLV-IV explosive compound for the first time in a delivery system smaller than a mortar round. The same size as a normal grenade, the IPE grenade delivers a greater blast than conventional explosives, at the same weight.

	Concealability	Damage	Weight	Blast Reduction	Cost
IPE Offensive	6	5S4	.25	−1 per 2 Meters	50¥
IPE Defensive	6	5S4	.25	−1 per Meter	50¥
IPE Concussion	6	5M3 Stun	.25	−1 per Meter	50¥
IPE Mini-Grenade	8	as above	.1	as appropriate	80¥

*If an explosive detonates in a room, any character standing inside could be subject to an overpressure effect. If there is still sufficient blast for an explosive shock-wave to pass a character, rebound off a nearby wall or wall-sized obstruction and reach him again, raise the Power Level of the explosive by 2. For example: Dave Danger is doing his thing in the Transit Authority Men's Room when a Thrill Gang member tosses an IPE concussion grenade in. The IPE grenade detonates two meters from Dave. The shockwave travels two meters to him, and then another meter to the wall beyond him. Rebounding, it travels the meter back to him. It has now traveled a total of 4 meters. Its Power Level is 5, and so Dave is subject to overpressure. Had the blast traveled more than 5 meters to hit him again, he would not be subject to it. Note that the blast of an offensive grenade can travel 10 meters (−1 per 2 meters) and still subject characters to overpressure. The Blast effect is always figured from the point where the blast first passes the target.

GYRO-MOUNT SYSTEM

ORDER HERE

SALESPERSON

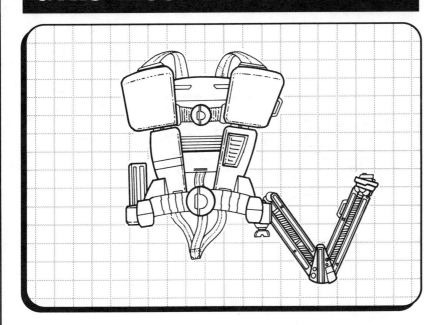

•Rugged, durable, precision gyroscopic stabilization!

This overbody, vest-style, gyro-stabilization system is perfect for those unwieldy weapons like the Ingram Valiant or the Ares MP Light Machine Gun. Consisting of an anchored shock harness and quick-detach battery cases, the Gyro-Mount System carries the weapon on an articulated arm attached to the shock harness at the waist. The weapon is mounted on the top of the gimbal arm and is capable of a full motion on three axes and through 160 degrees. The quad-cell battery system provides roughly three hours of continuous use at full load.

	Mount	Concealability	Rating	Weight	Cost
Gyro-Mount*	Under	−6	5	5	3,500¥
Deluxe Gyro	Under	−7	7	7	7,800¥

*The Improved Gyro-Mount will negate recoil as well as movement modifiers up to the rating indicated. The wearer has access to one-half his normal Dodge Pool, has no Defense Pool, and receives an additional +4 modifier to any attempt to engage in melee combat.

>>>>>[Hey, here's a neat trick to try. Put one of these on, pop your MP Light Machine Gun on top, and then run real fast. Sure, the gun stays nice and level, even at full-auto, but then try to turn. That's right, just a little side-step or two. Yeah, that's right. The gyros want to negate any kind of motion, even yours. Think of that when you're looking to hose the local slicer-dicer gang.]<<<<<
—Steel Lynx <17:48:23/12-21-50>

67

ORDER HERE

SALESPERSON

SECTION

2

ARES

RANGEFINDER GRENADE LINK

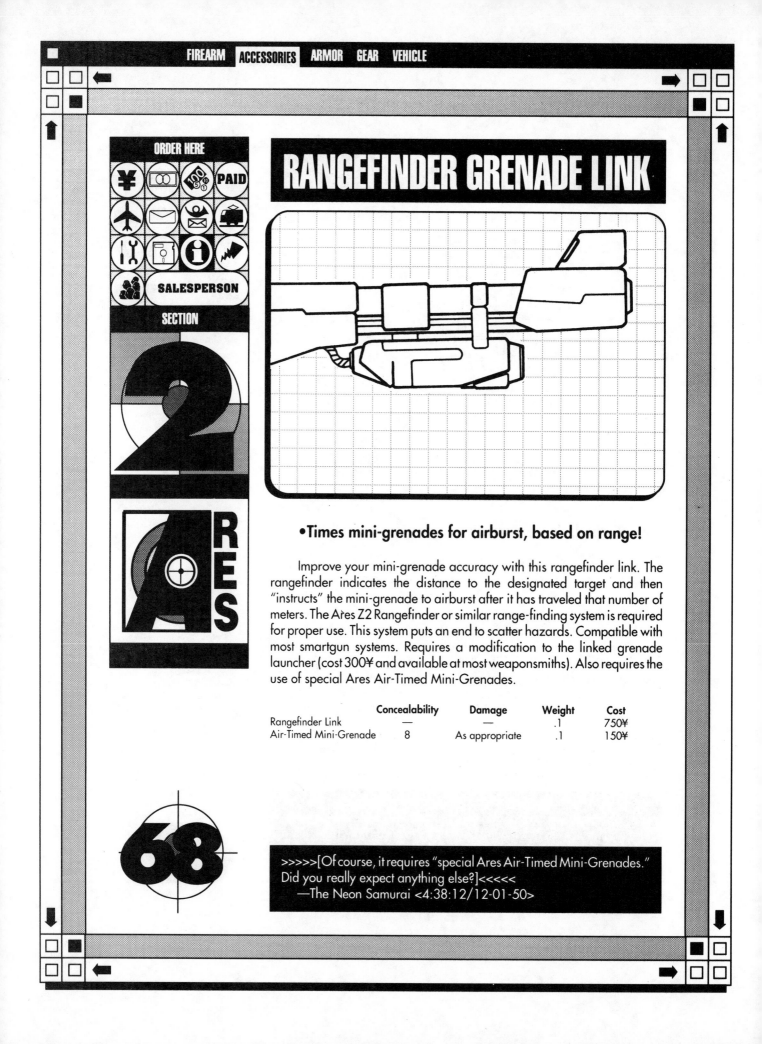

•Times mini-grenades for airburst, based on range!

Improve your mini-grenade accuracy with this rangefinder link. The rangefinder indicates the distance to the designated target and then "instructs" the mini-grenade to airburst after it has traveled that number of meters. The Ares Z2 Rangefinder or similar range-finding system is required for proper use. This system puts an end to scatter hazards. Compatible with most smartgun systems. Requires a modification to the linked grenade launcher (cost 300¥ and available at most weaponsmiths). Also requires the use of special Ares Air-Timed Mini-Grenades.

	Concealability	Damage	Weight	Cost
Rangefinder Link	—	—	.1	750¥
Air-Timed Mini-Grenade	8	As appropriate	.1	150¥

68

>>>>>[Of course, it requires "special Ares Air-Timed Mini-Grenades." Did you really expect anything else?]<<<<<
—The Neon Samurai <4:38:12/12-01-50>

RIOT-SECURITY SHIELD

ORDER HERE

PAID

SALESPERSON

•Crystal-clear high-impact plasteel construction!

The Ares Personal Riot-Security Shield is the ultimate in see-through riot-security defense. Designed to be used one-handed, either right or left, the R-S Shield is perfect for street use or for high-threat situations when an additional degree of mobile protection is necessary. The R-S Shield is available in two sizes, small and large. The small shield is a half-body type ideal for use with standard police/security gear. It fits snugly into the trunk of most standard police/security cruisers. The large shield is designed for riot control and high-threat operations. Fully portable, it has been designed for easy deployment from most squad vehicles.

	Ballistic	Dodge	Weight	Cost
Small R-S Shield	1	2	2	1,500¥
Large R-S Shield	2	3	3	3,200¥

*Ballistic Armor is cumulative with the armor of the user. The Dodge Rating is the number of additional Dodge Pool dice the defender receives. Additionally, the defender receives a +2 modifier to melee attacks when carrying an R-S Shield. If used to bash, the shield has a damage code of (Str÷2)L2.

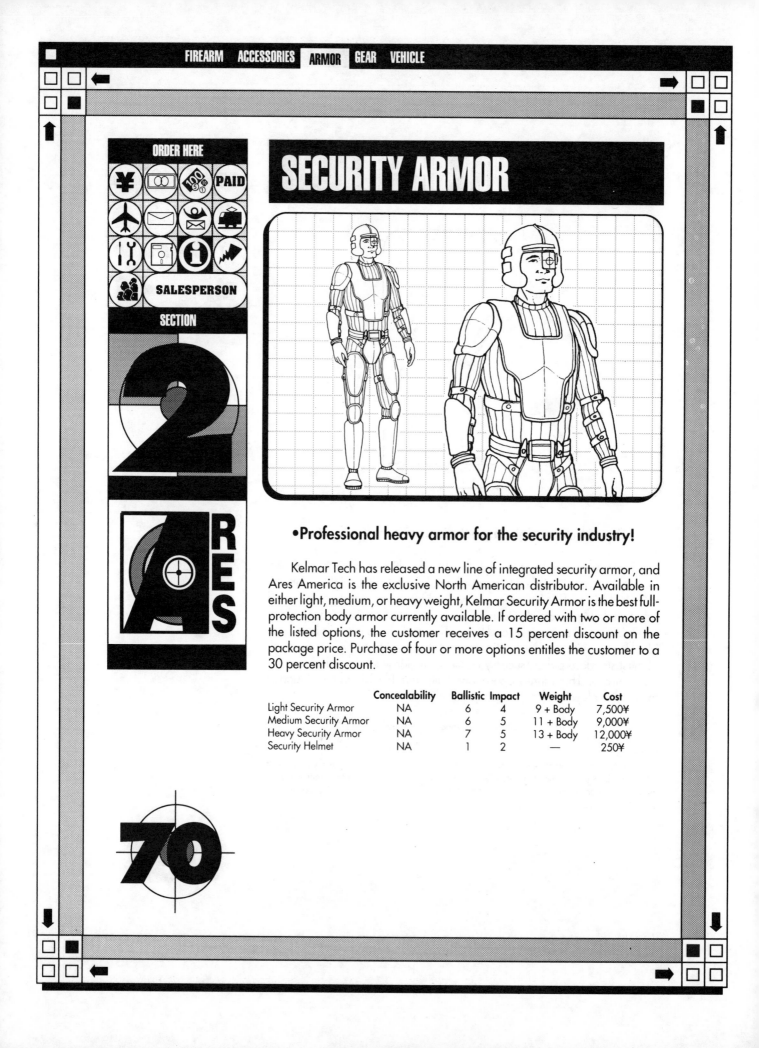

ORDER HERE

SALESPERSON

SECTION

2

SECURITY ARMOR

•Professional heavy armor for the security industry!

Kelmar Tech has released a new line of integrated security armor, and Ares America is the exclusive North American distributor. Available in either light, medium, or heavy weight, Kelmar Security Armor is the best full-protection body armor currently available. If ordered with two or more of the listed options, the customer receives a 15 percent discount on the package price. Purchase of four or more options entitles the customer to a 30 percent discount.

	Concealability	Ballistic	Impact	Weight	Cost
Light Security Armor	NA	6	4	9 + Body	7,500¥
Medium Security Armor	NA	6	5	11 + Body	9,000¥
Heavy Security Armor	NA	7	5	13 + Body	12,000¥
Security Helmet	NA	1	2	—	250¥

70

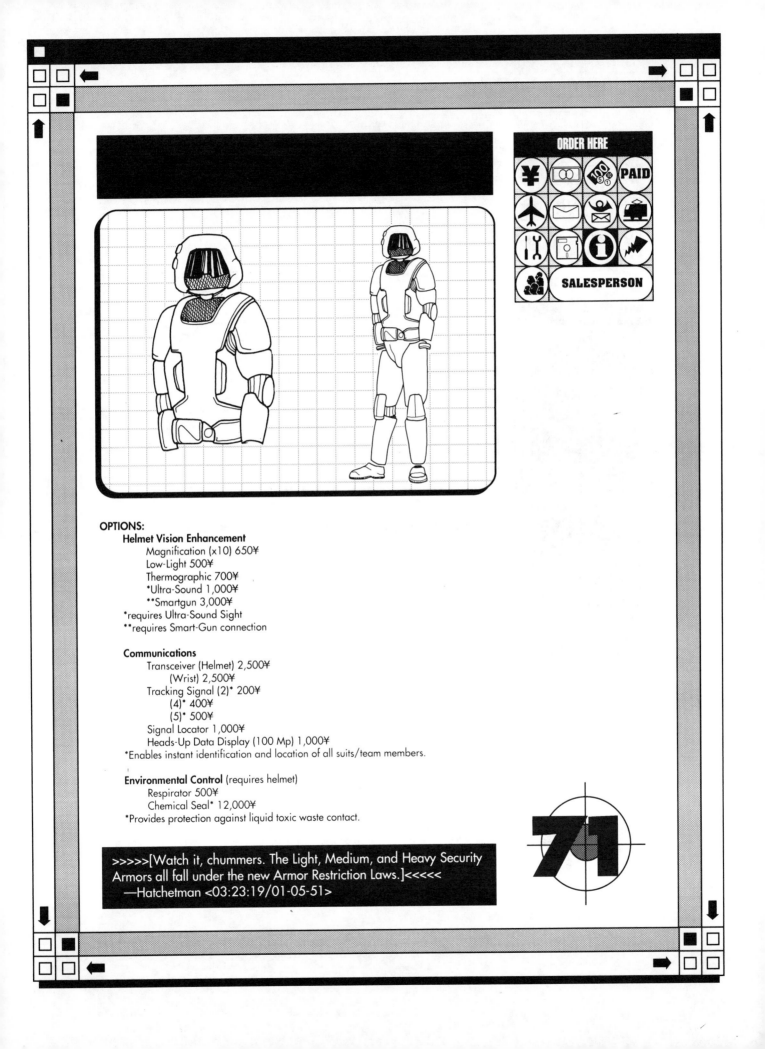

OPTIONS:

Helmet Vision Enhancement

Magnification (x10) 650¥
Low-Light 500¥
Thermographic 700¥
*Ultra-Sound 1,000¥
**Smartgun 3,000¥

*requires Ultra-Sound Sight
**requires Smart-Gun connection

Communications

Transceiver (Helmet) 2,500¥
(Wrist) 2,500¥
Tracking Signal (2)* 200¥
(4)* 400¥
(5)* 500¥
Signal Locator 1,000¥
Heads-Up Data Display (100 Mp) 1,000¥

*Enables instant identification and location of all suits/team members.

Environmental Control (requires helmet)

Respirator 500¥
Chemical Seal* 12,000¥

*Provides protection against liquid toxic waste contact.

>>>>>[Watch it, chummers. The Light, Medium, and Heavy Security Armors all fall under the new Armor Restriction Laws.]<<<<<
—Hatchetman <03:23:19/01-05-51>

71

ORDER HERE

SALESPERSON

SECTION

2

ARES

72

NET-GUN

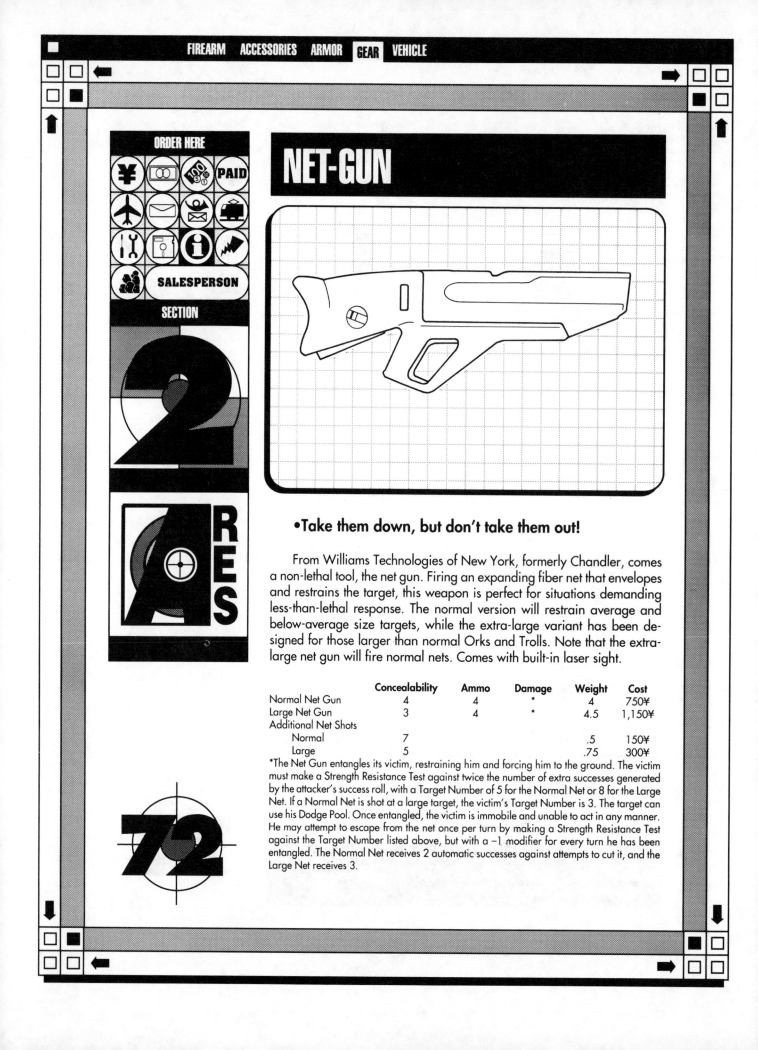

•Take them down, but don't take them out!

From Williams Technologies of New York, formerly Chandler, comes a non-lethal tool, the net gun. Firing an expanding fiber net that envelopes and restrains the target, this weapon is perfect for situations demanding less-than-lethal response. The normal version will restrain average and below-average size targets, while the extra-large variant has been designed for those larger than normal Orks and Trolls. Note that the extra-large net gun will fire normal nets. Comes with built-in laser sight.

	Concealability	Ammo	Damage	Weight	Cost
Normal Net Gun	4	4	*	4	750¥
Large Net Gun	3	4	*	4.5	1,150¥
Additional Net Shots					
Normal	7			.5	150¥
Large	5			.75	300¥

*The Net Gun entangles its victim, restraining him and forcing him to the ground. The victim must make a Strength Resistance Test against twice the number of extra successes generated by the attacker's success roll, with a Target Number of 5 for the Normal Net or 8 for the Large Net. If a Normal Net is shot at a large target, the victim's Target Number is 3. The target can use his Dodge Pool. Once entangled, the victim is immobile and unable to act in any manner. He may attempt to escape from the net once per turn by making a Strength Resistance Test against the Target Number listed above, but with a −1 modifier for every turn he has been entangled. The Normal Net receives 2 automatic successes against attempts to cut it, and the Large Net receives 3.

RIOT-CONTROL VEHICLE

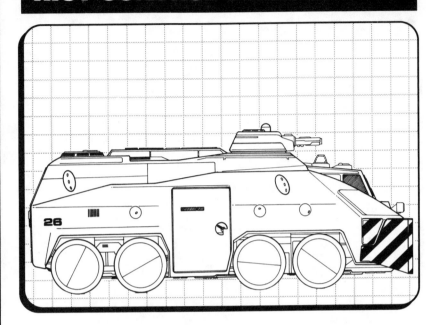

•Beyond a doubt, the ultimate urban security vehicle!

Based on the popular Ares Citymaster chassis, the Armored Riot-Control Vehicle can fulfill all urban security needs. Not only is the basic vehicle an upgrade of the Citymaster design, but add-on packages are available to adapt the vehicle to the needs of your particular urban situation. The Armored Riot-Control vehicle comes with a dual-mount roof-turret hardpoint and a pair of side gas-grenade launchers. The vehicle is set up to act as a command post and staging base for up to ten riot-equipped troops, but other configurations are available on request.

	Handling	Speed	Body	Signature	Pilot	Cost
ARC Vehicle	4	40/120	5	5	5	3 650 000¥
			Effect			Cost
Handling Packages			(–1 Handling)			+70,000¥
			(–2 Handling)			+160,000¥
Improved Engine			(50/150 speed)			+90,000¥
Structural Upgrades			(+1 Body)			+95,000¥
			(+2 Body)			+198,000¥
Improved Armor			(+1 Armor; –10% base speed)			+170,000¥
			(+2 Armor; –20% base speed)			+250,000¥
Improved Signature			(-1 Signature)			+85,000¥
			(-2 Signature)			+145,000¥
AutoPilot Upgrades			(+1 Pilot)			+50,000¥
			(+2 Pilot)			+120,000¥

73

ORDER HERE

SALESPERSON

SECTION

2

RES

A

74

WASP and YELLOWJACKET

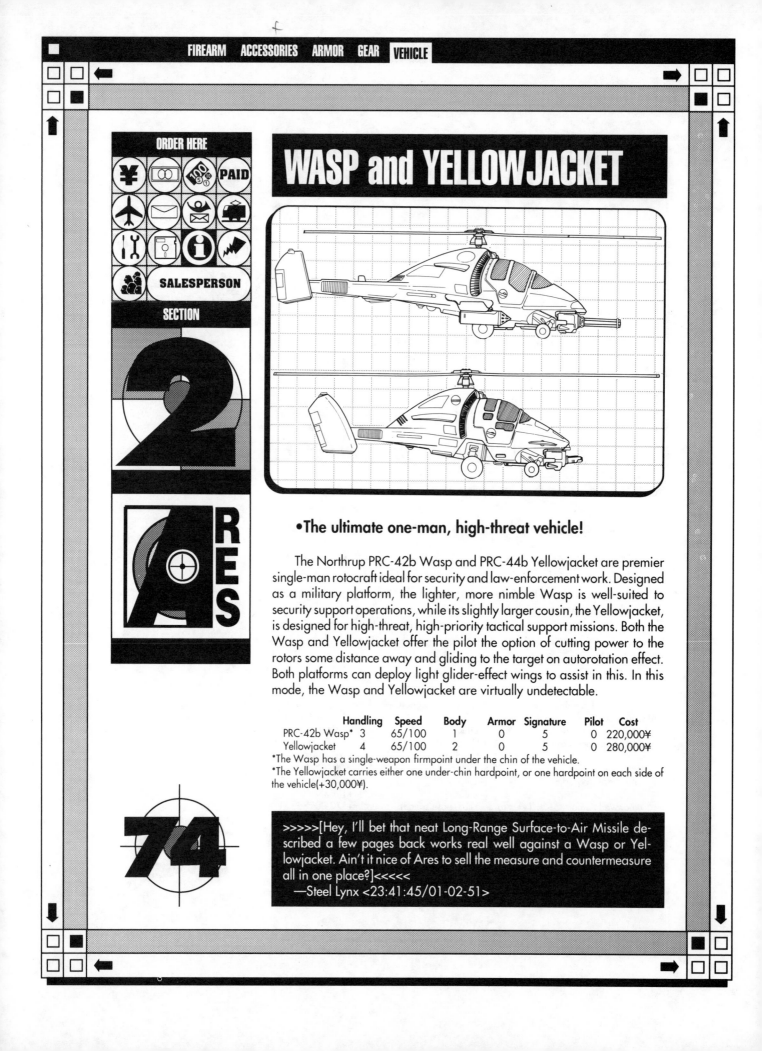

•The ultimate one-man, high-threat vehicle!

The Northrup PRC-42b Wasp and PRC-44b Yellowjacket are premier single-man rotocraft ideal for security and law-enforcement work. Designed as a military platform, the lighter, more nimble Wasp is well-suited to security support operations, while its slightly larger cousin, the Yellowjacket, is designed for high-threat, high-priority tactical support missions. Both the Wasp and Yellowjacket offer the pilot the option of cutting power to the rotors some distance away and gliding to the target on autorotation effect. Both platforms can deploy light glider-effect wings to assist in this. In this mode, the Wasp and Yellowjacket are virtually undetectable.

	Handling	Speed	Body	Armor	Signature	Pilot	Cost
PRC-42b Wasp*	3	65/100	1	0	5	0	220,000¥
Yellowjacket	4	65/100	2	0	5	0	280,000¥

*The Wasp has a single-weapon firmpoint under the chin of the vehicle.
*The Yellowjacket carries either one under-chin hardpoint, or one hardpoint on each side of the vehicle(+30,000¥).

>>>>>[Hey, I'll bet that neat Long-Range Surface-to-Air Missile described a few pages back works real well against a Wasp or Yellowjacket. Ain't it nice of Ares to sell the measure and countermeasure all in one place?]<<<<<
—Steel Lynx <23:41:45/01-02-51>

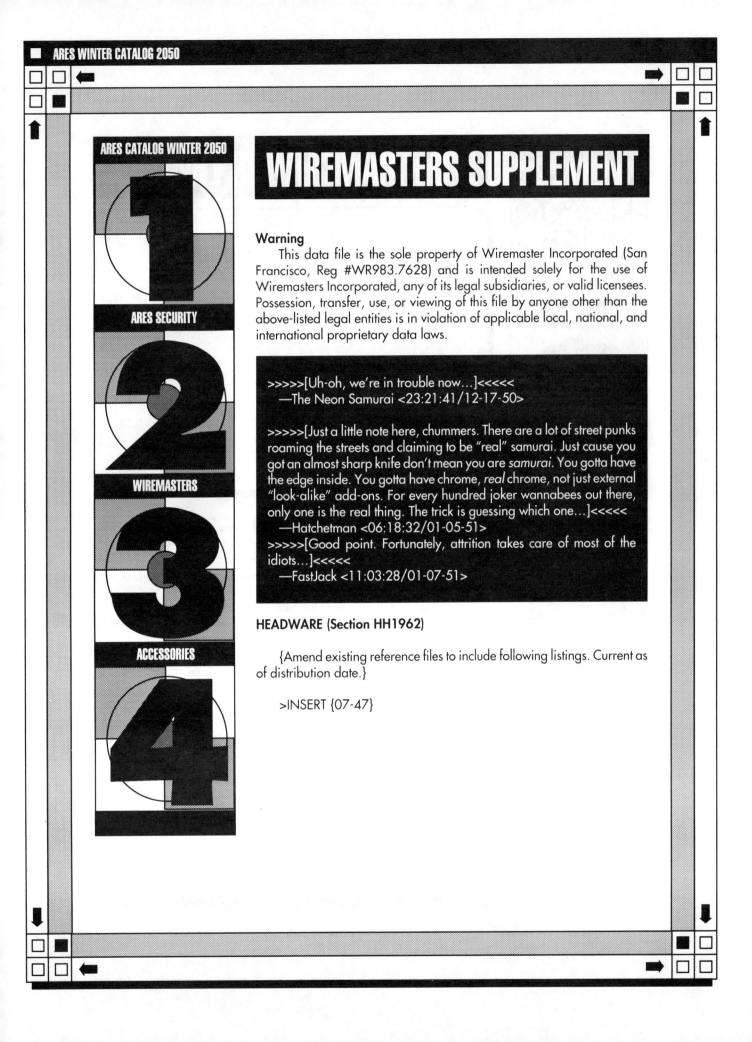

ARES CATALOG WINTER 2050

1

ARES SECURITY

2

WIREMASTERS

3

ACCESSORIES

4

WIREMASTERS SUPPLEMENT

Warning

This data file is the sole property of Wiremaster Incorporated (San Francisco, Reg #WR983.7628) and is intended solely for the use of Wiremasters Incorporated, any of its legal subsidiaries, or valid licensees. Possession, transfer, use, or viewing of this file by anyone other than the above-listed legal entities is in violation of applicable local, national, and international proprietary data laws.

>>>>>[Uh-oh, we're in trouble now...]<<<<<
—The Neon Samurai <23:21:41/12-17-50>

>>>>>[Just a little note here, chummers. There are a lot of street punks roaming the streets and claiming to be "real" samurai. Just cause you got an almost sharp knife don't mean you are *samurai*. You gotta have the edge inside. You gotta have chrome, *real* chrome, not just external "look-alike" add-ons. For every hundred joker wannabees out there, only one is the real thing. The trick is guessing which one...]<<<<<
—Hatchetman <06:18:32/01-05-51>
>>>>>[Good point. Fortunately, attrition takes care of most of the idiots...]<<<<<
—FastJack <11:03:28/01-07-51>

HEADWARE (Section HH1962)

{Amend existing reference files to include following listings. Current as of distribution date.}

>INSERT {07-47}

SECTION

3

WIRE MASTERS

COMMUNICATIONS LINK

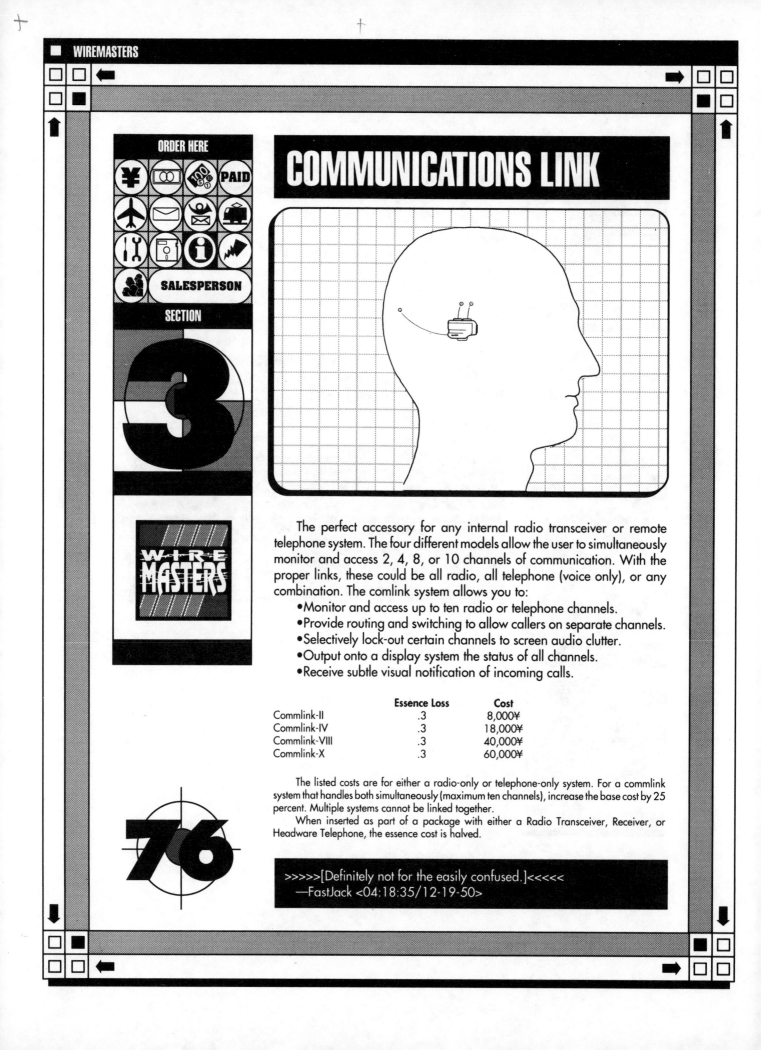

The perfect accessory for any internal radio transceiver or remote telephone system. The four different models allow the user to simultaneously monitor and access 2, 4, 8, or 10 channels of communication. With the proper links, these could be all radio, all telephone (voice only), or any combination. The comlink system allows you to:

- Monitor and access up to ten radio or telephone channels.
- Provide routing and switching to allow callers on separate channels.
- Selectively lock-out certain channels to screen audio clutter.
- Output onto a display system the status of all channels.
- Receive subtle visual notification of incoming calls.

	Essence Loss	Cost
Commlink-II	.3	8,000¥
Commlink-IV	.3	18,000¥
Commlink-VIII	.3	40,000¥
Commlink-X	.3	60,000¥

The listed costs are for either a radio-only or telephone-only system. For a commlink system that handles both simultaneously (maximum ten channels), increase the base cost by 25 percent. Multiple systems cannot be linked together.

When inserted as part of a package with either a Radio Transceiver, Receiver, or Headware Telephone, the essence cost is halved.

>>>>>[Definitely not for the easily confused.]<<<<<
—FastJack <04:18:35/12-19-50>

76

CRYPTO CIRCUIT HD

ORDER HERE

SALESPERSON

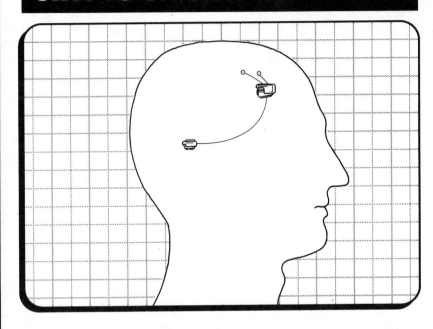

A Headware communications accessory, the Crypto Circuit HD allows transmission and reception of scramble-coded signals of varying levels of sophistication. Each signal transmitted by a Crypto Circuit system is layered with a sequenced code accessible only by other Crypto Circuit systems with the proper decoding sequence. The special code provides a potentially infinite variety of sequences.

This patented system is in use by military, governmental, and corporate security forces worldwide.

Crypto Circuit HD	Essence Loss	Cost
Level 1–4	.1	(Level) x 10,000¥
Level 5–7	.1	(Level) x 20,000¥
Level 8–9	.1	(Level) x 30,000¥
Level 10	.1	(Level) x 50,000¥

The Crypto Circuit HD is fully compatible with the commlink system and can provide coding and decoding functions for all channels. Both sender and receiver must be equipped with Crypto Circuit systems. The rating of the receiver's system must equal or exceed that of the sender.

The Crypto Circuit causes no Essence Loss when inserted as a package with either a Radio, Radio Receiver, or Headware Telephone system.

The Crypto Circuit system is also available for non-cyberware communication equipment at 50 percent of the listed price.

ORDER HERE

SALESPERSON

SECTION

3

WIRE MASTERS

HEARING AMPLIFICATION

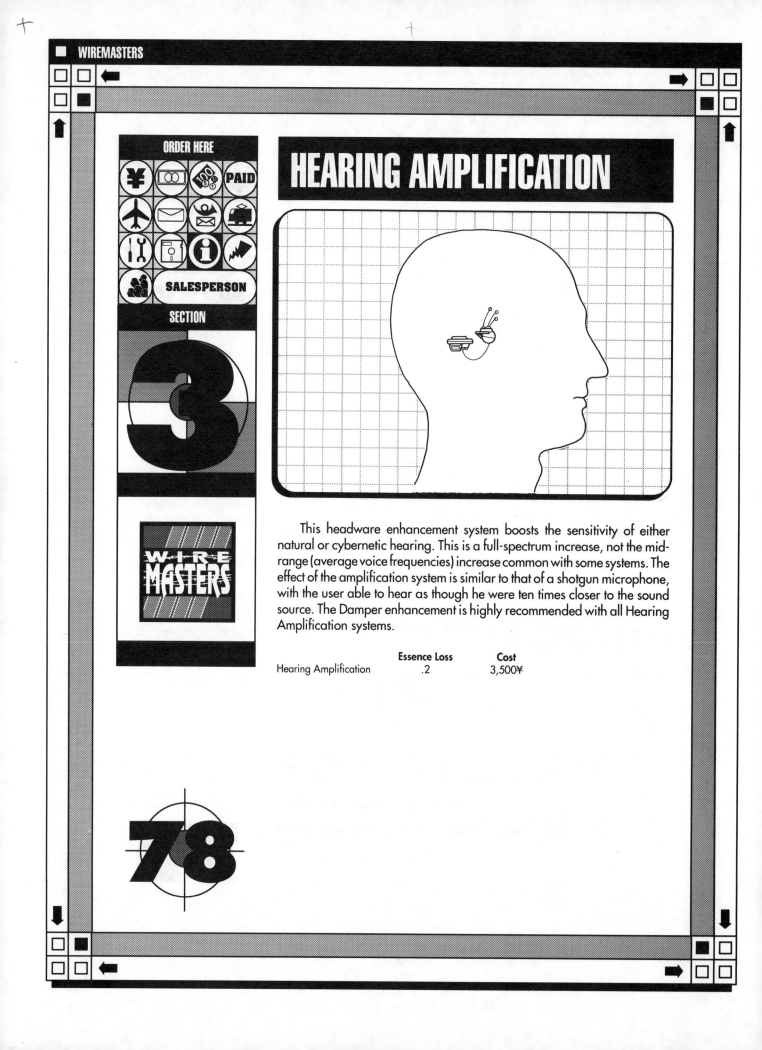

This headware enhancement system boosts the sensitivity of either natural or cybernetic hearing. This is a full-spectrum increase, not the mid-range (average voice frequencies) increase common with some systems. The effect of the amplification system is similar to that of a shotgun microphone, with the user able to hear as though he were ten times closer to the sound source. The Damper enhancement is highly recommended with all Hearing Amplification systems.

	Essence Loss	Cost
Hearing Amplification	.2	3,500¥

78

INTERNAL VOICE MASK

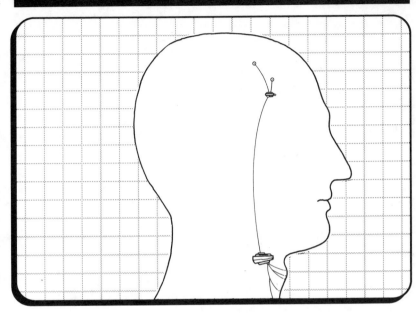

This cyber-speech accessory duplicates the operation of the external Voice Mask in every way, but with improved masking capability.

	Essence Loss	Rating	Cost
Internal Voice Mask	.1	2D6+2	7,000¥

>>>>>[Wow! Now I can sound like Governor Shultz! Or…or…Max Foley! Or…or…Neil the Ork Barbarian! Or…or…Holly Brighton! Or…or…Maria Mercurial! Or…or…Dunkelzahn The Dragon! (And get my own resort… and my own trideo show…and…and…)]<<<<<
—Findler-Man <21:09:14/12-19-50>
>>>>>[Excuse me?]<<<<<
—Dunkelzahn <02:17:51/12-28-50>
>>>>>[????]<<<<<
—FastJack <18:23:28/12-30-50>

RANGEFINDER

ORDER HERE

SALESPERSON

SECTION

3

WIRE MASTERS

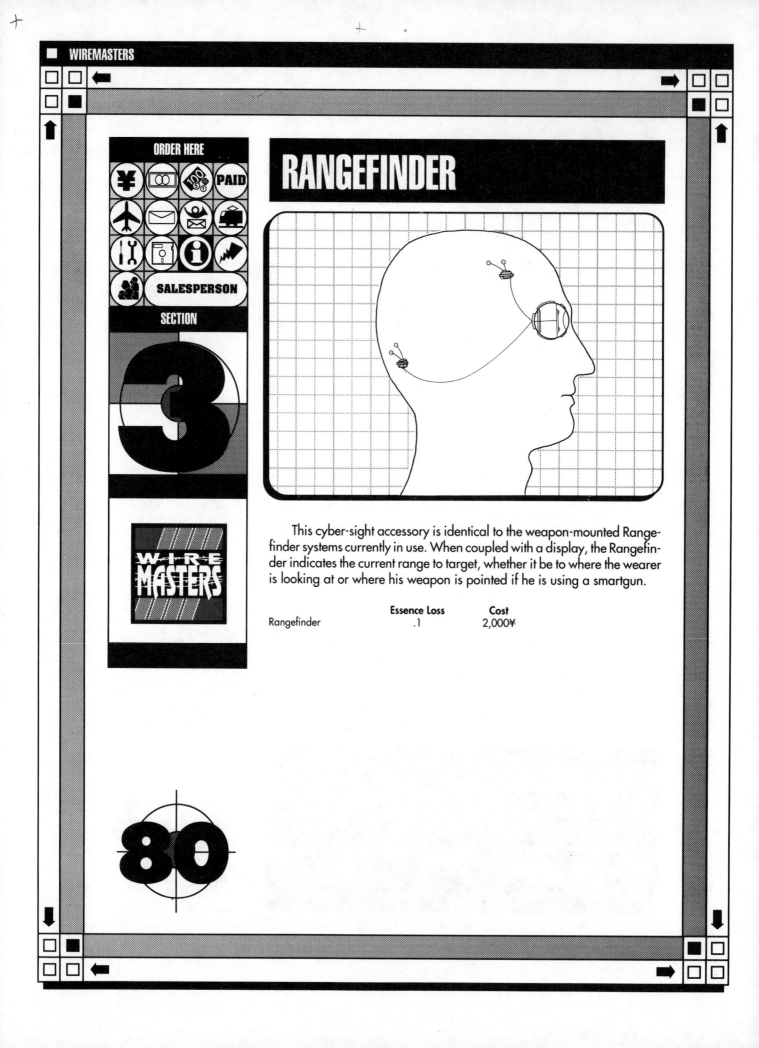

This cyber-sight accessory is identical to the weapon-mounted Rangefinder systems currently in use. When coupled with a display, the Rangefinder indicates the current range to target, whether it be to where the wearer is looking at or where his weapon is pointed if he is using a smartgun.

	Essence Loss	Cost
Rangefinder	.1	2,000¥

80

SCRAMBLE BREAKER HD

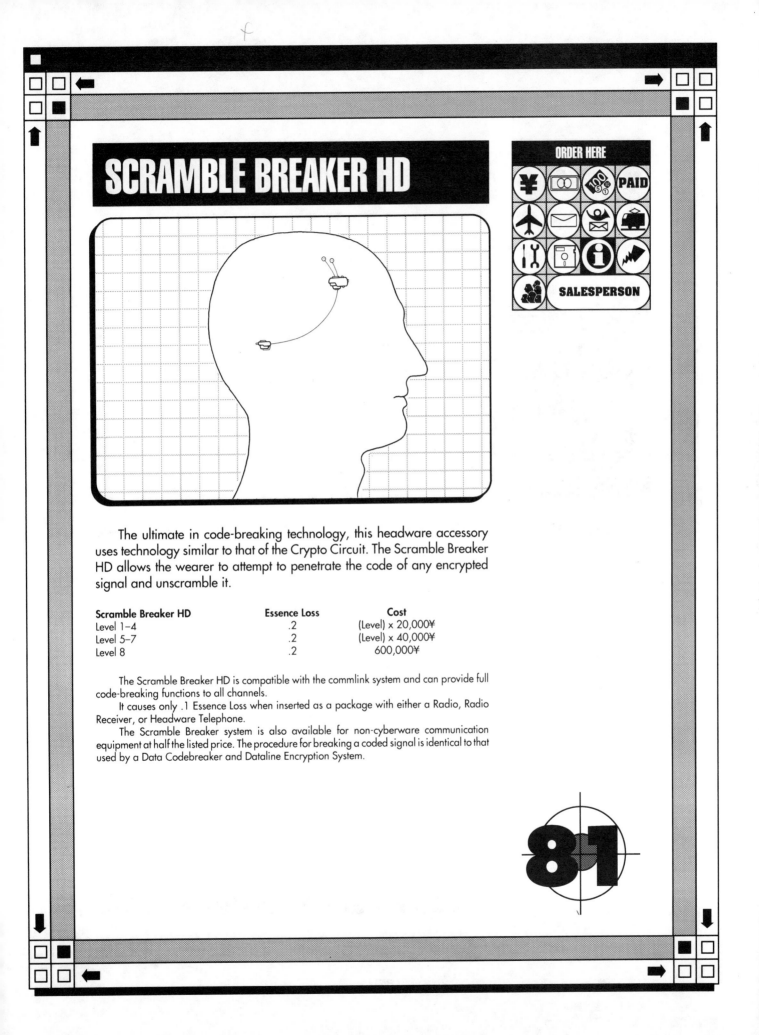

The ultimate in code-breaking technology, this headware accessory uses technology similar to that of the Crypto Circuit. The Scramble Breaker HD allows the wearer to attempt to penetrate the code of any encrypted signal and unscramble it.

Scramble Breaker HD	Essence Loss	Cost
Level 1–4	.2	(Level) x 20,000¥
Level 5–7	.2	(Level) x 40,000¥
Level 8	.2	600,000¥

The Scramble Breaker HD is compatible with the commlink system and can provide full code-breaking functions to all channels.

It causes only .1 Essence Loss when inserted as a package with either a Radio, Radio Receiver, or Headware Telephone.

The Scramble Breaker system is also available for non-cyberware communication equipment at half the listed price. The procedure for breaking a coded signal is identical to that used by a Data Codebreaker and Dataline Encryption System.

81

ORDER HERE

¥ PAID

SALESPERSON

SECTION

3

WIRE MASTERS

SELECT SOUND FILTER

This audio accessory allows the user to selectively filter out certain sounds without affecting other sounds present. Uses would include filtering out environmental sounds in order to monitor a conversation more easily. The Select Sound Filter system comes in a variety of grades of technical sophistication and is compatible with all cyber-hearing systems and accessories.

	Essence Loss	Level	Cost
Sound Filter	.2	1–5	Level x 10,000¥

To use the Select Sound Filter, the user must make an Unresisted Success Test. He rolls dice equal to the filter's Rating against a Target Number based on the amount of noise the user wishes to filter compared to the total amount of noise present. If the noise to be filtered is only 10 percent of the sound present, the Target Number would be 2 or 3. If, on the other hand, it was 90 percent of the total sound present, it could be as high as 10 or 11. Fifty percent would be about 6. The exact numbers depend on the circumstances and the sounds involved. Louder sounds are far more difficult to filter than softer ones.

82

>>>>>[I am here to say that I have successfully used this wondrous device to filter out the rantings of my lady-love during one of her frequent "get a real life" tirades. A heart-felt "10" from me.]<<<<<
—The Neon Samurai <13:14:24/12-12-50>

SENSE LINK

ORDER HERE

SALESPERSON

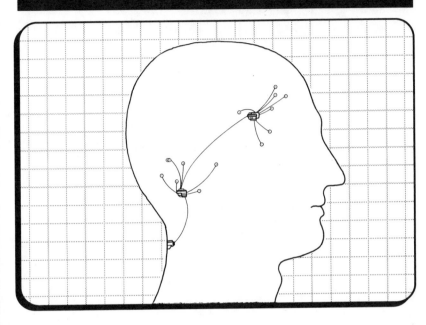

The Sense Link system is a basic Simulated Senses (Simsense) recording rig made affordable. Consisting of a series of phased neural sensors, the Sense Link can record and transmit the basic sensory impressions the wearer is receiving. The Sense Link can record full spectrum sight, sound, smell, taste, and touch, but does not record the wearer's emotions or attitudes. The Sense Link impression can be transmitted or recorded at a rate of 10Mp per 10 seconds of impressions. A Simsense player or cyberdeck is necessary to play back the recorded sensory impressions. Only a cyberdeck has the necessary electronics to play back a Sense Link transmission in real time.

	Essence Loss	Concealability	Cost
Sense Link	2	NA	300,000¥
Internal Transmitter	.6	NA	80,000¥
Sense Link Receiver*	NA	3	90,000¥
External Transmitter	NA	4	30,000¥
External Recorder	NA	6	1,500¥
(without memory)			

*Can only be attached to a cyberdeck or modified simsense player (non-portable).

>>>>>[Oh, the possibilities...]<<<<<
—Findler-Man <21:13:32/12-18-50>

ORDER HERE

¥ PAID

SALESPERSON

SECTION

3

WIRE MASTERS

VIDEO LINK

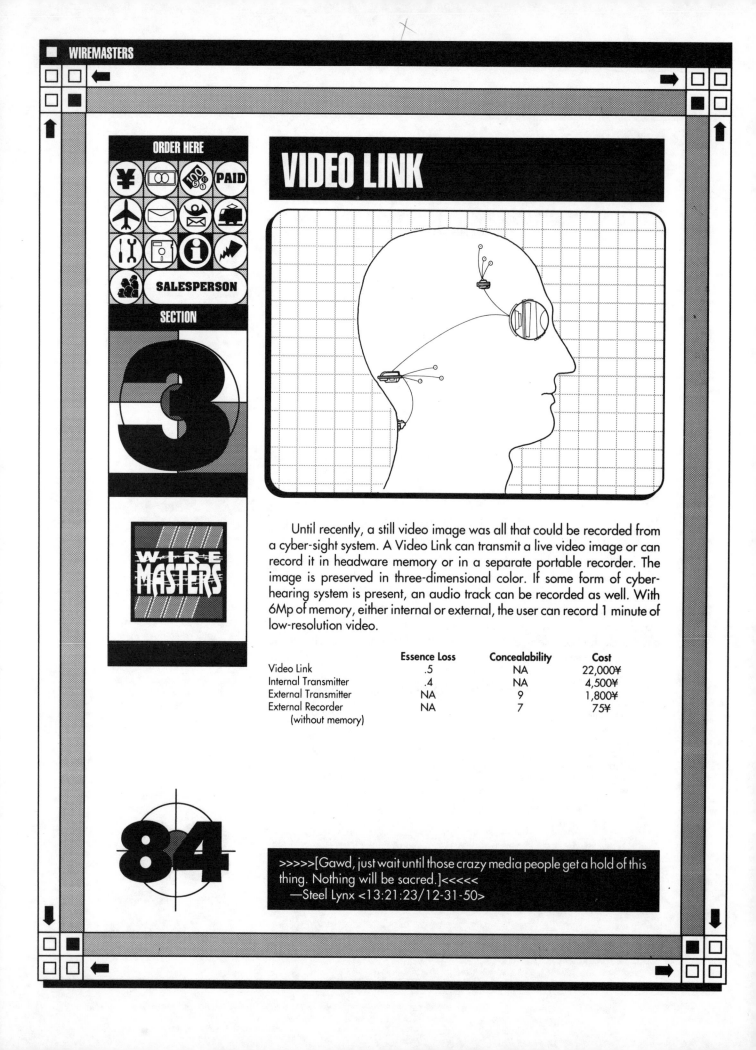

Until recently, a still video image was all that could be recorded from a cyber-sight system. A Video Link can transmit a live video image or can record it in headware memory or in a separate portable recorder. The image is preserved in three-dimensional color. If some form of cyber-hearing system is present, an audio track can be recorded as well. With 6Mp of memory, either internal or external, the user can record 1 minute of low-resolution video.

	Essence Loss	Concealability	Cost
Video Link	.5	NA	22,000¥
Internal Transmitter	.4	NA	4,500¥
External Transmitter	NA	9	1,800¥
External Recorder (without memory)	NA	7	75¥

>>>>>[Gawd, just wait until those crazy media people get a hold of this thing. Nothing will be sacred.]<<<<<
—Steel Lynx <13:21:23/12-31-50>

VISION MAGNIFICATION

ORDER HERE

SALESPERSON

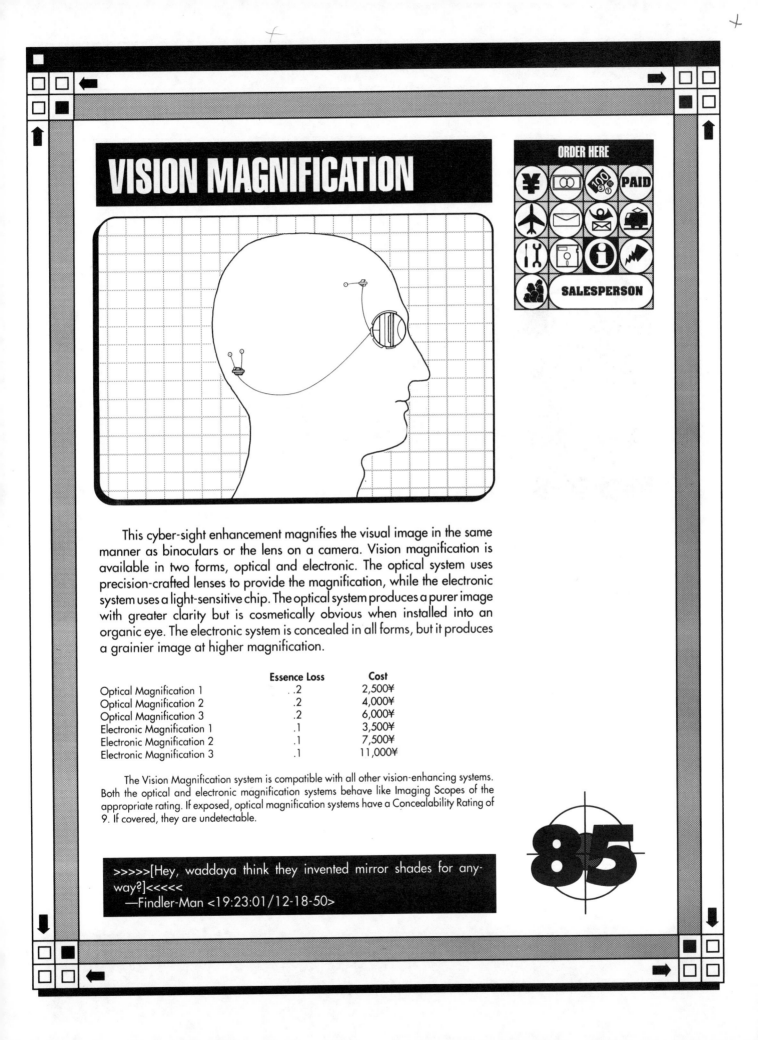

This cyber-sight enhancement magnifies the visual image in the same manner as binoculars or the lens on a camera. Vision magnification is available in two forms, optical and electronic. The optical system uses precision-crafted lenses to provide the magnification, while the electronic system uses a light-sensitive chip. The optical system produces a purer image with greater clarity but is cosmetically obvious when installed into an organic eye. The electronic system is concealed in all forms, but it produces a grainier image at higher magnification.

	Essence Loss	Cost
Optical Magnification 1	.2	2,500¥
Optical Magnification 2	.2	4,000¥
Optical Magnification 3	.2	6,000¥
Electronic Magnification 1	.1	3,500¥
Electronic Magnification 2	.1	7,500¥
Electronic Magnification 3	.1	11,000¥

The Vision Magnification system is compatible with all other vision-enhancing systems. Both the optical and electronic magnification systems behave like Imaging Scopes of the appropriate rating. If exposed, optical magnification systems have a Concealability Rating of 9. If covered, they are undetectable.

85

>>>>>[Hey, waddaya think they invented mirror shades for any-way?]<<<<<
—Findler-Man <19:23:01/12-18-50>

ORDER HERE

SALESPERSON

SECTION

3

WIRE MASTERS

CYBERGUNS

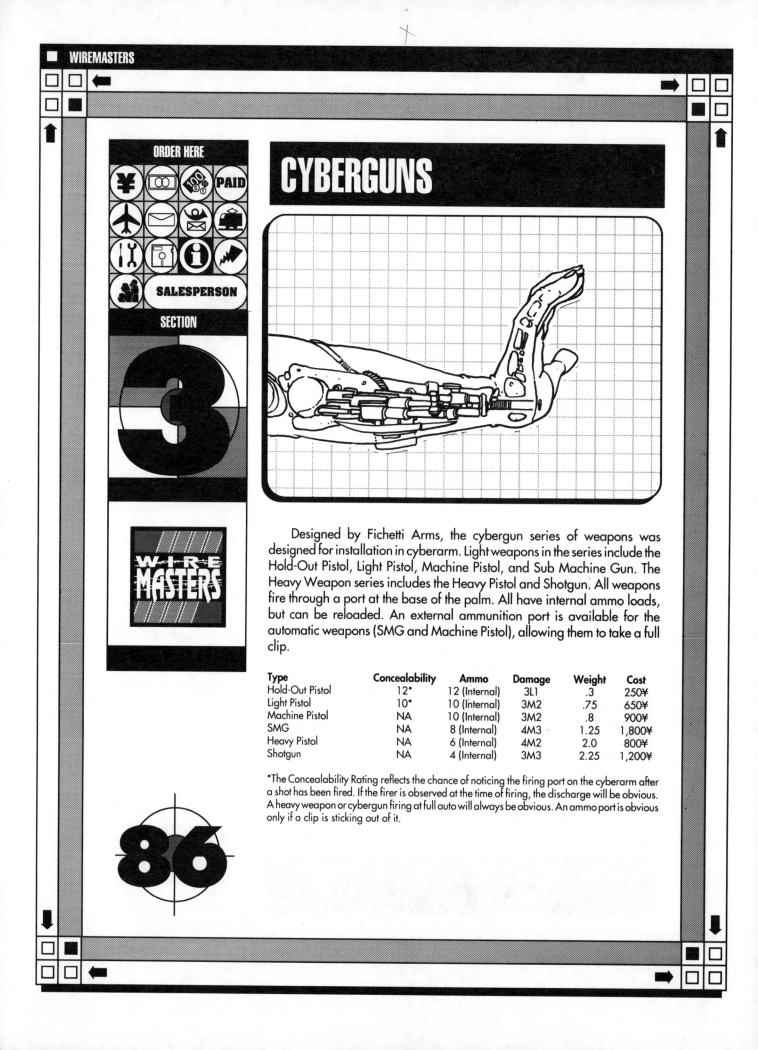

Designed by Fichetti Arms, the cybergun series of weapons was designed for installation in cyberarm. Light weapons in the series include the Hold-Out Pistol, Light Pistol, Machine Pistol, and Sub Machine Gun. The Heavy Weapon series includes the Heavy Pistol and Shotgun. All weapons fire through a port at the base of the palm. All have internal ammo loads, but can be reloaded. An external ammunition port is available for the automatic weapons (SMG and Machine Pistol), allowing them to take a full clip.

Type	Concealability	Ammo	Damage	Weight	Cost
Hold-Out Pistol	12*	12 (Internal)	3L1	.3	250¥
Light Pistol	10*	10 (Internal)	3M2	.75	650¥
Machine Pistol	NA	10 (Internal)	3M2	.8	900¥
SMG	NA	8 (Internal)	4M3	1.25	1,800¥
Heavy Pistol	NA	6 (Internal)	4M2	2.0	800¥
Shotgun	NA	4 (Internal)	3M3	2.25	1,200¥

*The Concealability Rating reflects the chance of noticing the firing port on the cyberarm after a shot has been fired. If the firer is observed at the time of firing, the discharge will be obvious. A heavy weapon or cybergun firing at full auto will always be obvious. An ammo port is obvious only if a clip is sticking out of it.

86

BOOSTED REFLEXES

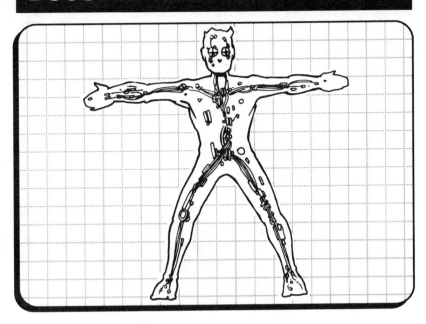

This one-time electro-chemical treatment and modification increases the body's natural reflexes without the need for cybernetic response amplifiers and neural-enhancement circuitry. The recipient of Boosted Reflexes, however, can never use Wired Reflexes or a Vehicle Control Rig. Boosted Reflexes cannot be upgraded.

Boosted Reflexes	Essence Loss	Reaction	Initiative	Cost
Level 1	.5	—	+1D6	15,000¥
Level 2	1.25	+1	+1D6	40,000¥
Level 3	2.8	+2	+2D6	90,000¥

>>>>[Great, just what we need.]<<<<<
—Findler-man<23:21:42/12-17-50>

ORDER HERE

SALESPERSON

SECTION

3

WIRE MASTERS

SKILL HARDWIRES

New Biofiber technology allows the permanent grafting of skill responses to an existing organic neuromuscular system. A Skill Hardwire can replicate any active, non-knowledge/information-based skill. Once installed, the Skill Hardwire is permanent and should never need maintenance within the user's lifetime.

		Essence Loss	Cost
Skill Hardwire	1–4	.2 x Rating	Rating x 5,000¥
	5–8	.25 x Rating	Rating x 50,000¥
	9–10	.3 x Rating	Rating x 500,000¥

(Can only be used for Active, Concentrated Skills, not Science, Mental, Social, or Magical Skills. Each Skill Hardwire is good for only 1 Skill and can never be changed, altered, upgraded, or modified. The Skill chosen must be a Concentration. General Skills and Specializations are not permitted.)

IMPROVED HAND RAZORS

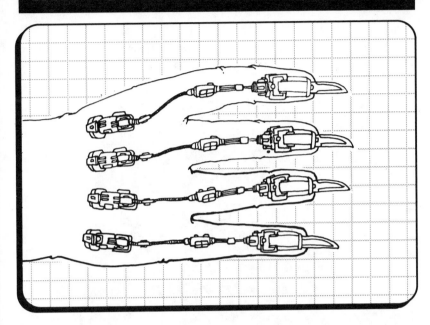

Wiremasters is proud to offer the new Wilkerson compression carbide blade replacements for Hand Razors. These replacement blades will fit all existing cyber-razor units currently manufactured. Please indicate manufacturer and model number when ordering.

	Damage	Cost
Improved Hand Razor	(Str)L2	8,500¥

(To upgrade to the new blades, simply contact a Street Doc, or other appropriate individual, and pay your money. The replacement takes 20 minutes.)

>>>>>[Hey, has anybody out there been able to figure out why a bunch of deckers are commenting on stuff we'll never have any use for? Just thought I'd ask.]<<<<<
—The Neon Samurai <15:31:32/12-19-50>
>>>>>[Because somebody has to?]<<<<<
—FastJack <23:12:31/12-21-50>
>>>>>[Because we're really vile, malicious, back-stabbing, rumormongers at heart?]<<<<<
—Findler-Man <03:42:45/12-23-50>
>>>>>[I'll buy that.]<<<<<
—NightFire <14:31:42/12-24-50>
>>>>>[You would. You get paid enough. Oh and hey, Merry Christmas.]<<<<<
—FastJack <02:33:16/12-25-50>

OPTIONAL RULES

INFORMATION

SALESPERSON

SECTION

4

APPENDICES

WORKING THE STREETS

—Abridged from an article by the same name, written by William "Wedge" Harkwood, first published in the June 2050 issue of *Street Fighting Man*.

BLAM! A single gunshot and another all-too-wise razorboy gets geeked. Why? Because he was stupid. Because he thought he knew best. Because he refused to listen.

Every punker that hits the streets thinks he knows best. He thinks he's got the ultimate edge and that everybody else will just fold up when he pops those long chromium carbide blades. Wrong. They're going to laugh instead.

The moment you step out on the streets, you must immediately assume that you are in a war zone and that you are a target. On the street, paranoia is a way of life. Without it, you're pizza. Assume that every situation, every deal, is potentially life-threatening and you just might live to see the morning.

There is no clean and fast way to work the streets. Nobody has a patented method of survival, but keeping certain things in mind just might make life a little safer.

Assume that everything you do is part of your own personal little war. All this drek about "Zenning" through life is garbage. Might as well put a bag over your head and dance in traffic.

Think about what you are doing. Plan ahead. Study your options. Try to out-think your opponent. Consider what he's going to do next, and what you can do to be ready for it.

Know your enemy. By learning all you can about him, you can begin to understand how he thinks and is likely to react. Knowledge is power.

Always check with your Contacts. Even if the deal looks so clean it squeaks, check it out. Even if it's your big-buddy older-brother sliding it to you, check it out. I'm not saying you should always believe everything you hear, but put your ear to the pavement and listen anyway.

Pay attention to your surroundings. Know your territory. Too many young razorboys assume they can get away with carrying their Kingslayer Assault Cannons casually over one shoulder while window-shopping along Money Street.

Laws and enforcement vary, depending where you are. Procedures can change from block to block and from cop to cop. If you're in a neighborhood that the cops like, play it safe, take it easy, and keep it concealed. The worse the neighborhood, the more the cops are going to let things slide. A heavy weapon of any kind is an excuse to call out the riot squad, and an assault rifle is worth at least three carloads of back-up, and maybe even a light chopper.

INFORMATION

SALESPERSON

SECTION

4

APPENDICES

Carrying big guns and obvious armor is just asking for trouble, in any neighborhood. In many places, an obvious weapon or obvious armor make you an immediate target.

Understand how this war of yours is going to be fought. It serves no purpose to have your H&K 227 in perfect working order if your enemy is going to shut you down with long-range magic. Study the options, consider the possibilities.

It also serves no purpose to take on an obviously superior foe head-on. Use hit-and-run tactics whenever possible. Keep your engagements short and sharp. Use the shock of violence to your advantage and be gone before that shock wears off. Leave the protracted open-field fighting to the military idiots who have the manpower to soak up the casualties.

If you do get into combat, try to get out of it as fast as you can. There is too much uncertainty in the chaos of battle to guarantee any result. If you must fight, control it. Choose the terrain, choose the weaponry, choose the participants.

Do not let your opponent set the pace. Be active, not reactive. Force his hand, rather than letting him force yours. Gain and hold the initiative.

Harass your opponent. Anger may lead to error.

The only thing you can be certain of is what you can do. Everything else is suspect.

And never, ever, be dumb enough to think you've won.

CYBERWARE DAMAGE

Don't'cha just hate it when that happens?
—Kid Stealth

At some point, the unthinkable always occurs. It may be the result of a particularly lethal blast of autofire, a former friend's wandering monowhip, or the front bumper of a barrelling CityMaster. Either way, sometime, somewhere, when you least desire it, your cyberware is gonna get *broke*.

How can this happen?, you ask. Very easily, comes the reply. Whenever a cyberware-bearing body takes traumatic damage, there is a chance, based on the severity of the wound, that one or more pieces of cyberware will become damaged and dysfunctional. In **Shadowrun**, a traumatic wound is any *single* wound of Serious or Deadly severity. That Serious or Deadly wound must be from one bullet, one blow, or one zap of magic, and it must be *physical* damage.

DETERMINING SYSTEM DAMAGE

When a Serious Wound is done, roll 1D6 and subtract 4. If the wound was Deadly, roll 1D6 and subtract only 2. The result is the number of *potential* cybersystems that might be damaged as a result of the wound. Roll that number of times against the table that follows. First, roll 1D6 to determine what type system took damage, and then roll 2D6 to identify the specific system.

DAMAGE TABLES

Determine System Type

	1D6
Headware	1–3
Bodyware	4–6

Determine Specific System

Headware	2D6
Cybereye	1–3
Data/Chipjack	4–5
Memory System	6–7
Other Cybersystem	8–9
Cyberear	10–12

Bodyware	2D6
Cyberarm	1–3
Reflex Modifier	4–6
Skillwire System	7–8
Other Cybersystem	9
Cyberleg	10–12

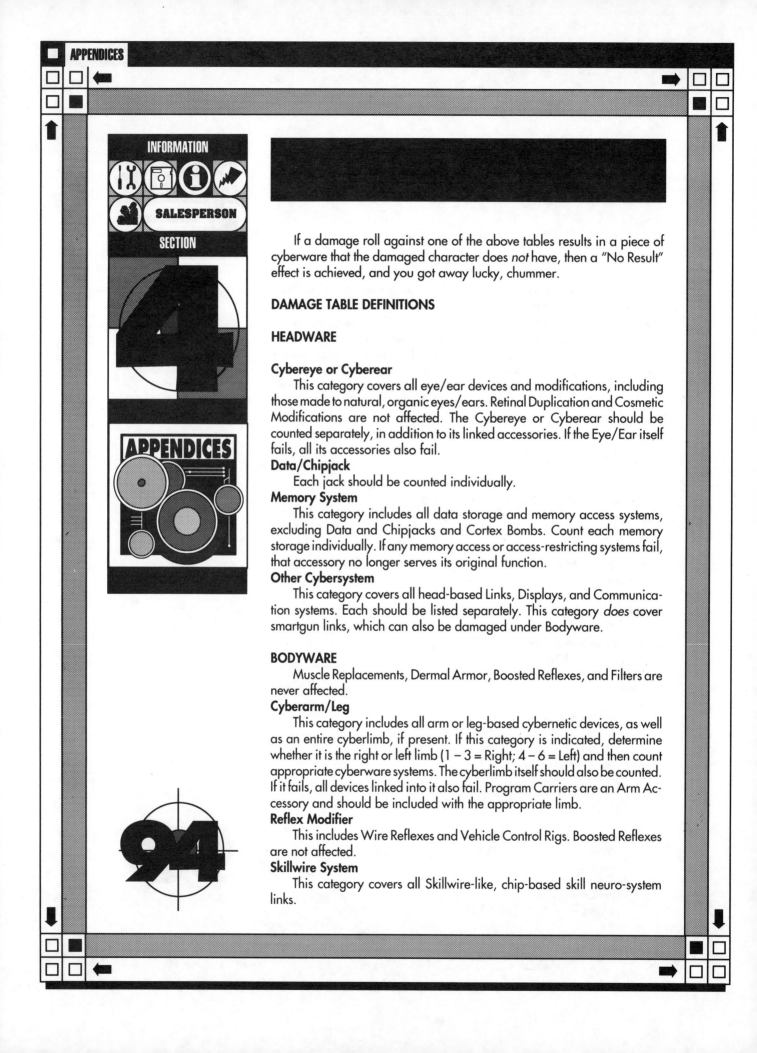

INFORMATION

SALESPERSON

SECTION

4

APPENDICES

If a damage roll against one of the above tables results in a piece of cyberware that the damaged character does *not* have, then a "No Result" effect is achieved, and you got away lucky, chummer.

DAMAGE TABLE DEFINITIONS

HEADWARE

Cybereye or Cyberear
This category covers all eye/ear devices and modifications, including those made to natural, organic eyes/ears. Retinal Duplication and Cosmetic Modifications are not affected. The Cybereye or Cyberear should be counted separately, in addition to its linked accessories. If the Eye/Ear itself fails, all its accessories also fail.

Data/Chipjack
Each jack should be counted individually.

Memory System
This category includes all data storage and memory access systems, excluding Data and Chipjacks and Cortex Bombs. Count each memory storage individually. If any memory access or access-restricting systems fail, that accessory no longer serves its original function.

Other Cybersystem
This category covers all head-based Links, Displays, and Communication systems. Each should be listed separately. This category *does* cover smartgun links, which can also be damaged under Bodyware.

BODYWARE
Muscle Replacements, Dermal Armor, Boosted Reflexes, and Filters are never affected.

Cyberarm/Leg
This category includes all arm or leg-based cybernetic devices, as well as an entire cyberlimb, if present. If this category is indicated, determine whether it is the right or left limb (1 – 3 = Right; 4 – 6 = Left) and then count appropriate cyberware systems. The cyberlimb itself should also be counted. If it fails, all devices linked into it also fail. Program Carriers are an Arm Accessory and should be included with the appropriate limb.

Reflex Modifier
This includes Wire Reflexes and Vehicle Control Rigs. Boosted Reflexes are not affected.

Skillwire System
This category covers all Skillwire-like, chip-based skill neuro-system links.

94

Other Cybersystem

This includes any and all systems not covered by one of the above categories, including cyberware mounted in odd places, and Speech and Voice modification systems.

Any Damaged system must be Repaired (see page 96). If the same system is damaged more than once before it is repaired, then it must be replaced.

If the damaged system is Second-Hand Cyberware, any damage to the system results in a complete loss of the cyberware, which must be fully replaced. (See **Upgrading Cyberware**)

Karma can be spent to purchase a re-roll if a damage result is undesirable. The cost is 1 Karma Point per re-roll. This can be repeated as often as the player wishes until he gets the desired result or else runs out of Karma.

DETERMINING SUBSYSTEM DAMAGE

The method for determining exactly which subsystems will be affected is different for each character. After determining which specific system has been affected, make a list of the character's various pieces of cyberware that fall under that category, using the following guidelines:

•If there is only one subsystem under the category, that system is damaged.

•If the category includes two systems, there is a 50 percent chance that either one will be affected. Roll 1D6. A 1–3 result damages System A; a 4–6 result damages System B.

•If there are three systems in the category, the chances are as follows: 1–2 result damages System A; 3–4 damages System B; 5–6 damages System C.

•If there are from four to six systems, the chances are:

1 = System A	4 = System D
2 = System B	5 = System E (if none, roll again)
3 = System C	6 = System F (if none, roll again)

•If there are more than six systems, the following may be used as a guideline:

Chart 1
1= System A
2= System B
3= System C
4= System D
5=System E
6= Roll on Chart 2

Chart 2
1= System G
2= System H (if none, roll again Chart 1)
3= System I (if none, roll again Chart 1)
4= System J (if none, roll again Chart 1)
5= System K (if none, roll again Chart 1)
6= System L (if none, roll again Chart 1)

INFORMATION

SALESPERSON

SECTION

4

APPENDICES

CYBER REPAIR

Sure I can fix it, but it's gonna cost ya.
—Street Doc Credo

When a piece of cyberware gets broken, odds are that its owner will want to have it fixed. (Walking around with broken cyberware dangling from one's body can be downright embarrassing!) A Technician (or anyone) with Biotech (B/R) can do the job. We'll be nice and assume that no real surgery is necessary.

The Base Time for repair of a piece of broken cyberware is equal to the Base Essence (unmodified Essence) Cost of the broken system, multiplied by 2 hours.

The repairer has a repair Target Number based on the severity of the wound that caused the original system failure. A Serious Wound has a Target Number of 4, a Deadly Wound of 8.

Use the modifier table given with the Build/Repair skill use description on pp. 153–4 of the **Shadowrun** basic rules.

If a repair is made on Alpha or Beta Grade Custom Cyberware, double the final Target Number for Alpha Grade and triple it for Beta Grade.

Each success generated reduces the repair time required. Divide the Base Time by the number of successes to determine the actual time.

The cost for the repair has two factors: Parts and Labor. If the wound is Serious, the Parts cost is equal to the cost of the original cyberware mutiplied by .15. If the wound is Deadly, its repair cost is equal to the original cost multiplied by .35.

Labor is based on the repairer's Skill Rating. The Base Charge is equal to 50¥ for each skill point per hour. So, a technician with a Skill Rating of 6 would charge 300¥ per hour for his services. Technicians with a facility up-to-date enough to warrant Superior on the Build/Repair Modifiers Table also charge an additional usage fee, usually an amount quadrupling his charge (x4).

The Labor charges assume that the character cannot fast-talk a friend into doing the fix for him. It is also conceivable that a Technician or Street Doc could charge far in excess of the base charges listed above. It is, after all, a seller's market.

UPGRADING CYBRWARE

UPGRADING OR REPLACING CYBERWARE

Whatsa matter, the old stuff ain't good enough no more?
—Lou Welby, Street Doc

At some point, you may want to upgrade the piece of cyberware you are currently wearing, or may have to replace it. In either case, the procedure is the same.

All cyberware upgrades or replacement procedures are Elective Surgery, as described on page 144 of the **Shadowrun** rules. No medical rolls are neccessary for the surgery itself, for we assume technology has progressed to a state where table deaths are very rare.

The attending physician (or whoever is performing the surgery) does make a roll to determine how well he performed the surgery. Good surgery can reduce Essence Cost, while sloppy surgery can increase it. The character performing the surgery must make a Biotech (B/R) Skill Roll against a Target equal to 10 minus the new Essence of the character undergoing surgery. His new Essence is the rating he receives if the current surgery occurs without difficulties. After the Surgery Roll, consult the Essence Cost Table, below.

ESSENCE COST TABLE

No Successes	+15% Essence
1 Successes	+10% Essence
2–3 Successes	no change
4–5 Successes	−10% Essence
6 or greater	−20% Essence

Apply the percentage listed to the Essence Cost to determine the actual Essence Cost. If the Essence Cost would leave the character with Essence of less than 0, surgery will be suspended prior to death, the cyberware left uninstalled, and the character's Essence at 0.

As an option, the gamemaster may choose not to inform the player of his character's current new Essence. In this case, the player would only know what his Essence is as a result of successful surgery. It is then his option to take any further risks with additional surgery down the line.

INFORMATION

SALESPERSON

SECTION

4

APPENDICES

CUSTOM CYBERWARE

It may be good, but there's always better.
—Dr. Aidan Jarmani

Nothing gleams brighter than custom chrome. Go deep enough into the cities of Chiba, San Francisco, Brussels, Tel Aviv, Manhattan, Oslo, or Seattle, and you'll find them: Shadow Clinics.

A Shadow Clinic is the place to obtain the best, smoothest, slickest, and most expensive cyberware available. Most of it is not even made from recognizable technology, but it works. The name Shadow Clinic comes from the fact that they're unlicensed and underground, existing deep in the shadows. The established medical profession definitely disapproves of the "experimental medicine" they practice.

So, what exactly can custom cyberware do for a character? First, it is better quality, usually some bio-technological metaconstruct, meaning it costs less Essence. It is also more resistant to damage, but far more difficult to repair.

The Shadow Clinics to which the characters are most likely to have access offer basic levels of Custom Cyberware: Alpha and Beta, with Alpha being the cheaper, less-efficient grade.

	Essence Reduction	Cost Multiple	Damage Resist
Alpha	−20% (x.8)	x3	5/6
Beta	−40% (x.6)	x7	4/5

ESSENCE REDUCTION

Reduce the amount of Base Essence Cost by the percentage listed (or use the Multiple given in parenthesis.) Round all numbers up. Essence Cost may never be reduced below .05 in this manner.

COST MULTIPLE

Multiply the cost for the cyberware by the number indicated. Remember that this is only the cost for the actual piece of hardware, and does not include doctor's fees and hospitalization.

DAMAGE RESISTANCE

The first number given is the target for resisting damage from Serious Wounds, and the second from Deadly Wounds. When a piece of custom cyberware is damaged, roll 5 dice against the Target Number indicated above. Only one success is neccessary for the damage to be ignored completely.

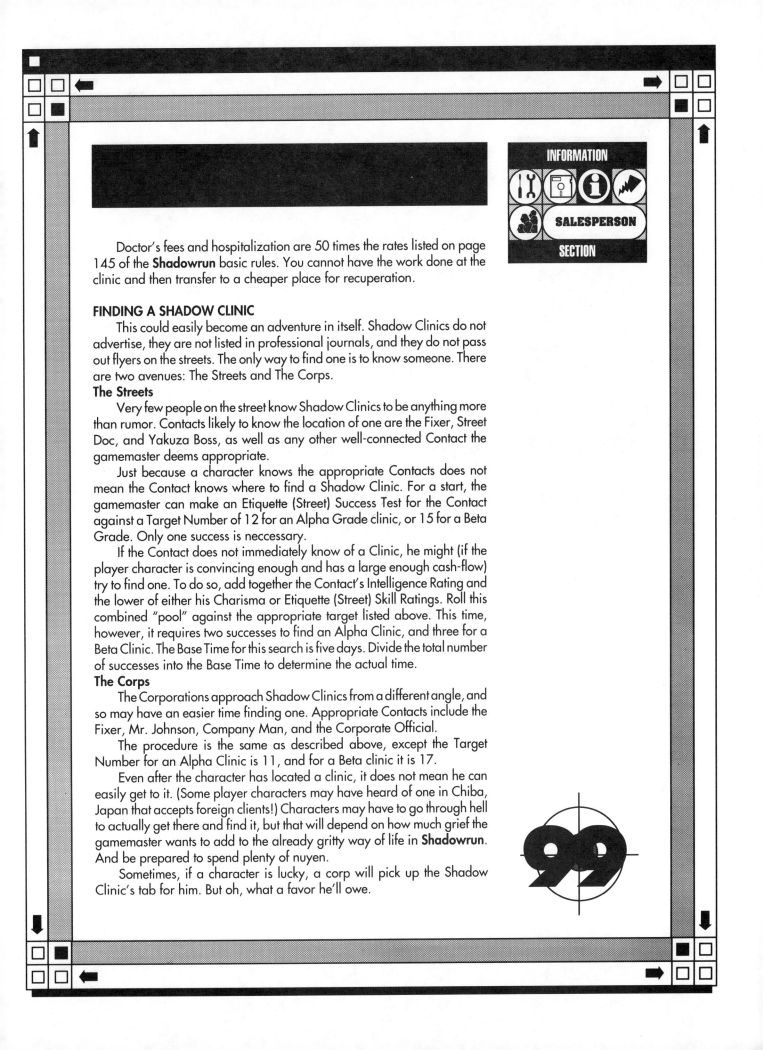

Doctor's fees and hospitalization are 50 times the rates listed on page 145 of the **Shadowrun** basic rules. You cannot have the work done at the clinic and then transfer to a cheaper place for recuperation.

FINDING A SHADOW CLINIC

This could easily become an adventure in itself. Shadow Clinics do not advertise, they are not listed in professional journals, and they do not pass out flyers on the streets. The only way to find one is to know someone. There are two avenues: The Streets and The Corps.

The Streets

Very few people on the street know Shadow Clinics to be anything more than rumor. Contacts likely to know the location of one are the Fixer, Street Doc, and Yakuza Boss, as well as any other well-connected Contact the gamemaster deems appropriate.

Just because a character knows the appropriate Contacts does not mean the Contact knows where to find a Shadow Clinic. For a start, the gamemaster can make an Etiquette (Street) Success Test for the Contact against a Target Number of 12 for an Alpha Grade clinic, or 15 for a Beta Grade. Only one success is neccessary.

If the Contact does not immediately know of a Clinic, he might (if the player character is convincing enough and has a large enough cash-flow) try to find one. To do so, add together the Contact's Intelligence Rating and the lower of either his Charisma or Etiquette (Street) Skill Ratings. Roll this combined "pool" against the appropriate target listed above. This time, however, it requires two successes to find an Alpha Clinic, and three for a Beta Clinic. The Base Time for this search is five days. Divide the total number of successes into the Base Time to determine the actual time.

The Corps

The Corporations approach Shadow Clinics from a different angle, and so may have an easier time finding one. Appropriate Contacts include the Fixer, Mr. Johnson, Company Man, and the Corporate Official.

The procedure is the same as described above, except the Target Number for an Alpha Clinic is 11, and for a Beta clinic it is 17.

Even after the character has located a clinic, it does not mean he can easily get to it. (Some player characters may have heard of one in Chiba, Japan that accepts foreign clients!) Characters may have to go through hell to actually get there and find it, but that will depend on how much grief the gamemaster wants to add to the already gritty way of life in **Shadowrun**. And be prepared to spend plenty of nuyen.

Sometimes, if a character is lucky, a corp will pick up the Shadow Clinic's tab for him. But oh, what a favor he'll owe.

INFORMATION

SALESPERSON

SECTION

4

APPENDICES

CHEAP CYBERWARE

BARGAIN BASEMENT CYBERWARE

I swear, a little old lady from Pasadena. Would I lie to you?
—Dynamic Dave, Cyber Salesman

Yes, it is possible to get second-hand cyberware. It costs 50 percent less, but is prone to breakage. Installation and Essence Cost are the same as for a normal piece of cyberware.

Second-hand cyberware does not necessarily break every time a character uses it—only when it is crucial that it not break. Once per adventure (and only once), the gamemaster may have the player make a Resistance Test for the piece of cyberware. Roll 5 dice against a Target Number of 4, modified by circumstance as the gamemaster sees fit. (For example, if it is a cheap cyberarm and the character is dangling from it off a building, the Target Number could go as high as 8.) Normal Karma rules apply, but it costs 2 points of Karma per die re-rolled.

If the piece of second-hand cyberware fails, it must be replaced. No repair is possible.

The potential failure of a piece of cyberware should only be used to increase dramatic tension, and not to harass the players. It is quite possible that it would never be appropriate at any time during the adventure for a particular character to make a roll against that piece of cyberware. So be it.

This option should only be used to add fun to the game, and not as an excuse for sudden character mortality.

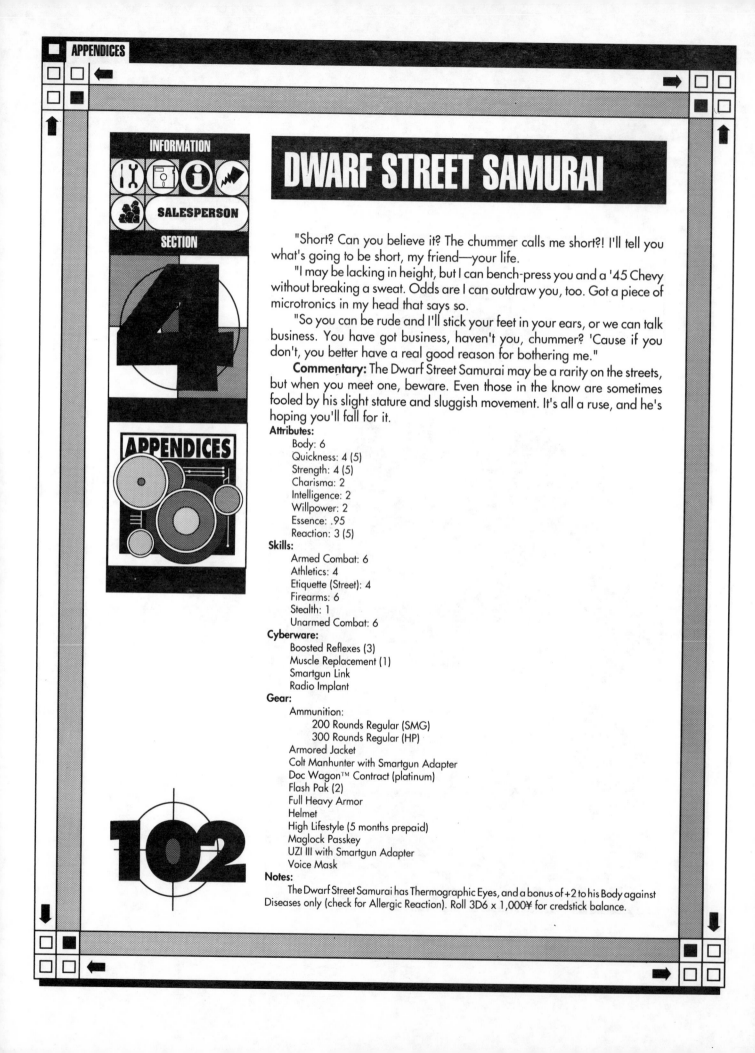

INFORMATION

SALESPERSON

SECTION

4

APPENDICES

DWARF STREET SAMURAI

"Short? Can you believe it? The chummer calls me short?! I'll tell you what's going to be short, my friend—your life.

"I may be lacking in height, but I can bench-press you and a '45 Chevy without breaking a sweat. Odds are I can outdraw you, too. Got a piece of microtronics in my head that says so.

"So you can be rude and I'll stick your feet in your ears, or we can talk business. You have got business, haven't you, chummer? 'Cause if you don't, you better have a real good reason for bothering me."

Commentary: The Dwarf Street Samurai may be a rarity on the streets, but when you meet one, beware. Even those in the know are sometimes fooled by his slight stature and sluggish movement. It's all a ruse, and he's hoping you'll fall for it.

Attributes:
Body: 6
Quickness: 4 (5)
Strength: 4 (5)
Charisma: 2
Intelligence: 2
Willpower: 2
Essence: .95
Reaction: 3 (5)

Skills:
Armed Combat: 6
Athletics: 4
Etiquette (Street): 4
Firearms: 6
Stealth: 1
Unarmed Combat: 6

Cyberware:
Boosted Reflexes (3)
Muscle Replacement (1)
Smartgun Link
Radio Implant

Gear:
Ammunition:
200 Rounds Regular (SMG)
300 Rounds Regular (HP)
Armored Jacket
Colt Manhunter with Smartgun Adapter
Doc Wagon™ Contract (platinum)
Flash Pak (2)
Full Heavy Armor
Helmet
High Lifestyle (5 months prepaid)
Maglock Passkey
UZI III with Smartgun Adapter
Voice Mask

Notes:
The Dwarf Street Samurai has Thermographic Eyes, and a bonus of +2 to his Body against Diseases only (check for Allergic Reaction). Roll 3D6 x 1,000¥ for credstick balance.

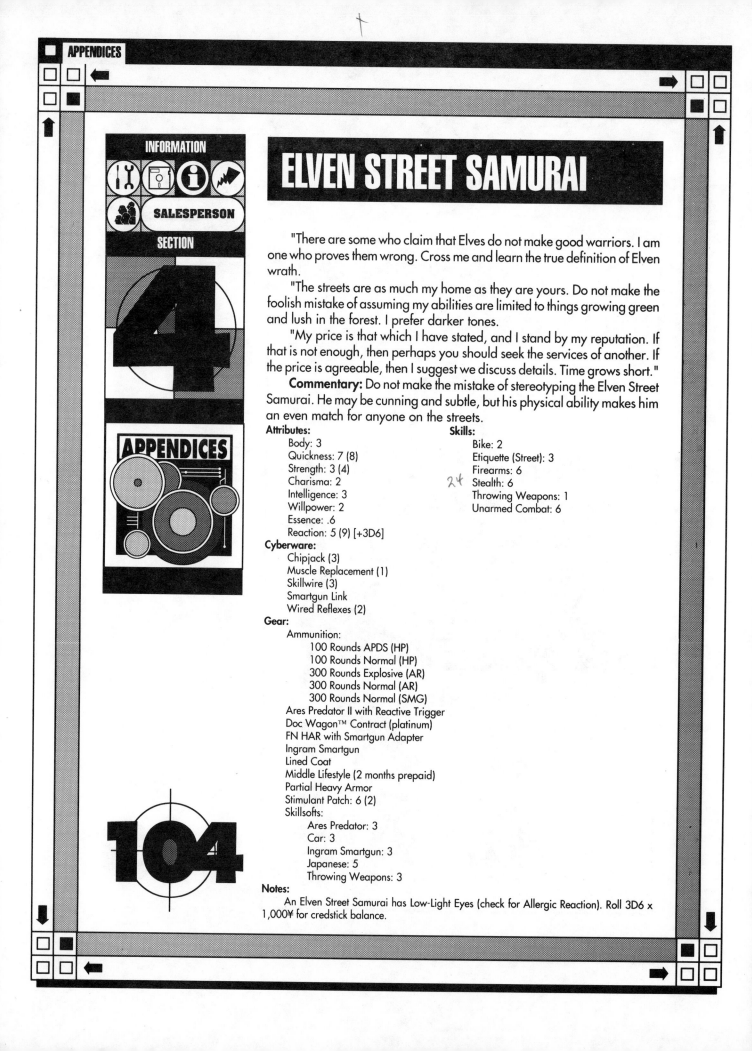

INFORMATION

SALESPERSON

SECTION

4

APPENDICES

ELVEN STREET SAMURAI

"There are some who claim that Elves do not make good warriors. I am one who proves them wrong. Cross me and learn the true definition of Elven wrath.

"The streets are as much my home as they are yours. Do not make the foolish mistake of assuming my abilities are limited to things growing green and lush in the forest. I prefer darker tones.

"My price is that which I have stated, and I stand by my reputation. If that is not enough, then perhaps you should seek the services of another. If the price is agreeable, then I suggest we discuss details. Time grows short."

Commentary: Do not make the mistake of stereotyping the Elven Street Samurai. He may be cunning and subtle, but his physical ability makes him an even match for anyone on the streets.

Attributes:
- Body: 3
- Quickness: 7 (8)
- Strength: 3 (4)
- Charisma: 2
- Intelligence: 3
- Willpower: 2
- Essence: .6
- Reaction: 5 (9) [+3D6]

Cyberware:
- Chipjack (3)
- Muscle Replacement (1)
- Skillwire (3)
- Smartgun Link
- Wired Reflexes (2)

Skills:
- Bike: 2
- Etiquette (Street): 3
- Firearms: 6
- Stealth: 6
- Throwing Weapons: 1
- Unarmed Combat: 6

2t

Gear:
- Ammunition:
  - 100 Rounds APDS (HP)
  - 100 Rounds Normal (HP)
  - 300 Rounds Explosive (AR)
  - 300 Rounds Normal (AR)
  - 300 Rounds Normal (SMG)
- Ares Predator II with Reactive Trigger
- Doc Wagon™ Contract (platinum)
- FN HAR with Smartgun Adapter
- Ingram Smartgun
- Lined Coat
- Middle Lifestyle (2 months prepaid)
- Partial Heavy Armor
- Stimulant Patch: 6 (2)
- Skillsofts:
  - Ares Predator: 3
  - Car: 3
  - Ingram Smartgun: 3
  - Japanese: 5
  - Throwing Weapons: 3

Notes:
An Elven Street Samurai has Low-Light Eyes (check for Allergic Reaction). Roll 3D6 x 1,000¥ for credstick balance.

INFORMATION

SALESPERSON

SECTION

4

APPENDICES

ORK STREET SAMURAI

"You seem surprised? Is it my clothing? The way I speak? Or is it the fact that I am Samurai?

"If you intend to work the street, you cannot be surprised. Surprise means weakness, and weakness spells death. You must learn to expect everything.

"And I expect you will find the conditions for my employment agreeable. Believe me, there is no one better suited than me. I am perfect for your shadowrun.

"Dere ain't nobody better who knows da streets like I's do. There, does that sound more Orkish for you?"

Commentary: Need to cut a deal with Orks? The Ork Street Samurai is your man. Need to cut a deal with anyone? The Ork Street Samurai is still your man.

Don't let the charming good looks or phony accent fool you. Beneath the smiling face is a street veteran, a tough professional who's lived through more trouble than you want to know. That's why he's smiling.

Because of his lack of cyberware, the Ork Street Samurai has a lighter touch than you would expect. He prefers more "organic" solutions.

Attributes:
  Body: 9
  Quickness: 4
  Strength: 6
  Charisma: 1
  Intelligence: 4
  Willpower: 3
  Essence: 5.2
  Reaction: 4

Skills:
  Armed Combat: 5
  Etiquette (Street): 3
  Firearms: 6
  Stealth: 2
  Unarmed Combat: 4

Cyberware:
  Retractable Spur
  Smartgun Link

Gear:
  AK-97 with Smartgun Adapter
  Ammunition:
      100 Rounds Normal (AR)
      100 Rounds Normal (HP)
  Ares Predator with Smartgun Adapter
  Armored Jacket
  Low Lifestyle (1 month prepaid)

Notes:
  The Ork Street Samurai has Natural Low-Light Eyes (check for Allergic Reaction). Roll 3D6 x 1,000¥ for credstick balance.

INFORMATION

SALESPERSON

SECTION

107

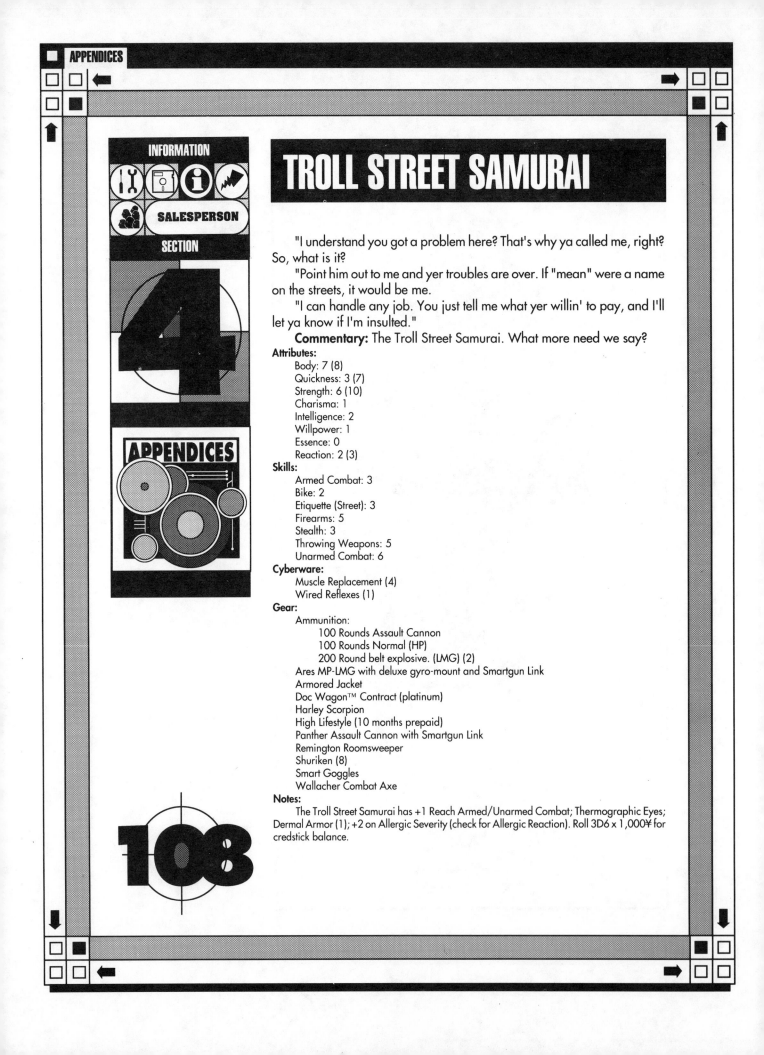

INFORMATION

SALESPERSON

SECTION

4

APPENDICES

TROLL STREET SAMURAI

"I understand you got a problem here? That's why ya called me, right? So, what is it?

"Point him out to me and yer troubles are over. If "mean" were a name on the streets, it would be me.

"I can handle any job. You just tell me what yer willin' to pay, and I'll let ya know if I'm insulted."

Commentary: The Troll Street Samurai. What more need we say?

Attributes:
Body: 7 (8)
Quickness: 3 (7)
Strength: 6 (10)
Charisma: 1
Intelligence: 2
Willpower: 1
Essence: 0
Reaction: 2 (3)

Skills:
Armed Combat: 3
Bike: 2
Etiquette (Street): 3
Firearms: 5
Stealth: 3
Throwing Weapons: 5
Unarmed Combat: 6

Cyberware:
Muscle Replacement (4)
Wired Reflexes (1)

Gear:
Ammunition:
100 Rounds Assault Cannon
100 Rounds Normal (HP)
200 Round belt explosive. (LMG) (2)
Ares MP-LMG with deluxe gyro-mount and Smartgun Link
Armored Jacket
Doc Wagon™ Contract (platinum)
Harley Scorpion
High Lifestyle (10 months prepaid)
Panther Assault Cannon with Smartgun Link
Remington Roomsweeper
Shuriken (8)
Smart Goggles
Wallacher Combat Axe

Notes:
The Troll Street Samurai has +1 Reach Armed/Unarmed Combat; Thermographic Eyes; Dermal Armor (1); +2 on Allergic Severity (check for Allergic Reaction). Roll 3D6 x 1,000¥ for credstick balance.

WEAPONRY

MELEE WEAPONS

Edged Weapons	Concealability	Reach	Damage	Weight	Cost
Ares Monosword	3	+1	(Str)M3	2	2,500¥
Centurion Laser Axe	2	+1	(Str)S2	5.2	3,500¥
Combat Axe	2	+2	(Str)S2	2.0	750¥
Thrusting point	NA	0	(Str ÷ 2)L3	—	—
Katana	3	+1	(Str)M3	1	1,000¥
Knife	8	0	(Str ÷ 2)L1	.5	30¥
Survival Knife	6	0	(Str)L3	.75	450¥
Sword	4	+1	(Str)M2	1	500¥
Pole Arms/Staffs					
Pole Arm	2	+2	(Str)S3	4	500¥
Staff	2	+2	(Str)M2 Stun	2	50¥
Clubs					
Club	5	+1	(Str + 1)M2 Stun	1	10¥
Defiance AZ-150 Stun Baton	5	+1	5L3 Stun*	1	1,500¥
Sap	8	0	(Str)M2 Stun	—	10¥
Stun Baton	4	+1	5L2 stun + special	1	750¥
Other					
Forearm Snap Blades	7	0	(Str)M2	1.5	850¥
Hand Razor	NA/10*	0	(Str ÷ 2)L2	—	4,500/9,000¥*
Improved Blade	NA/10*	0	(Str)L2	—	+8,500¥**
Shock Glove	9	0	5L3 Stun*	.5	950¥
Spurs	NA/9*	0	(Str)M2	—	7,000/11,500¥*

*Non-Retractable/Retractable
**Replacement Cost

Whips/Flails	Concealability	Reach	Damage	Weight	Cost
Monofilament Whip	10	+2	6S4	—	3,000¥

PROJECTILE WEAPONS

Bows	Concealability	Reach	Damage	Weight	Cost
Bow	3	NA	(Str)M2	1	300¥
Arrows	3	NA	as bow	.1	10¥
Ranger X Compound Bow	4	NA	(Str + 1)M2	1.5	550¥
Ranger X Precision Arrows	3	NA	as bow	.08	18¥
Crossbows					
Light	2	1	4L3	2	300¥
Medium	2	2	5M2	3	400¥
Heavy	NA	2	6S2	4	500¥
Bolts	4	NA	as crossbow	.05	5¥

THROWING WEAPONS

Non-Aerodynamic	Concealability	Reach	Damage	Weight	Cost
Throwing Knife	9	NA	(Str ÷ 2)L1	.25	20¥
Aerodynamic					
Shuriken	8	NA	(Str ÷ 2)L1	.25	30¥

FIREARMS

Pistols	Type	Concealability	Ammo	Damage	Weight	Cost
Streetline Special	Hold-out	8	6 (Clip)	3L1	.5	100¥
Tiffani Self-Defender	Hold-out	8	4 (Clip)	3L1	.5	450¥
Walther Palm Pistol	Hold-out	9	2 (Break)	3L1	.25	200¥
Ares Light Fire 70	Light	5	16 (Clip)	3M2	1	475¥
Beretta 200ST	Light	4	26 (Clip)	3M2	2	750¥
Beretta Model 101T	Light	5	10 (Clip)	3M2	1	350¥
Ceska vz/120	Light	7	18 (Clip)	3M2	1	500¥
Colt America L36	Light	6	9 (Clip)	3M2	1	350¥
Fichetti Security 500	Light	7	10 (Clip)	3M2	1	400¥
Fichetti Security 500	Light	6	22 (Clip)	3M2	1.25	450¥
Seco LD-120	Light	5	12 (Clip)	3M2	1	400¥
Ares Crusader MP	Light (MP)	6	40 (Clip)	3M2	3.25	950¥
Ceska Black Scorpion MP	Light (MP)	6	25 (Clip)	3M2	2.75	750¥
			35 (Clip)			
Ares Predator	Heavy	5	10 (Clip)	4M2	2.25	450¥
Ares Predator II	Heavy	4	15 (Clip)	6M2	2.5	550¥
Ares Viper Slivergun	Heavy	6	30 (Clip)	2M3	2	600¥
Browning Max-Power	Heavy	6	8 (Clip)	4M2	2	450¥
Browning Ultra-Power	Heavy	6	10 (Clip)	4M2	2.25	525¥
Colt Manhunter	Heavy	5	16 (Clip)	4M2	2.25	425¥
Remington Roomsweeper	Heavy	8	6 (Magazine)	3M3	2.5	500¥
Ruger Super Warhawk	Heavy	4	6 (Cylinder)	4M2	2.5	300¥
Narcoject Weapons						
Narcoject Pistol	Light	7	5 (Clip)	**	1.5	600¥
Narcoject Rifle	Shotgun	4	10 (Clip)	**	3.25	1,700¥

	Type	Concealability	Ammo	Damage	Weight	Cost
Rifles						
AK-97	Assault	3	22 (Clip)	5M3	4.5	700¥
AK-98	Assault	NA	22 (Clip)	5M3	6	2,500¥
Colt M22a2 Assault Rifle	Assault	3	40 (Clip)	5M3	4.75	1,600¥
FN HAR	Assault	2	20 (Clip)	5M3	4.5	1,200¥
Heckler & Koch G12A3z	Assault	2	32 (Clip)	5M3	5.25	2,200¥
Samopal vz88V	Assault	2	35 (Clip)	5M3	5.5	1,800¥
Steyr AUG-CSL	Assault	2	40 (Clip)	5M3	4	*
Remington 750	Sporting	3	5 (Magazine)	5S2	3	600¥
Remington 950	Sporting	2	5 (Magazine)	6S2	4	800¥
Ruger 100 Sporting Rifle	Sporting	2	5 (Magazine)	5S2	3.75	1,300¥
Steyr AUG-CSL Carbine	Sporting	3	40 (Clip)	5M3	3.75	*
Ranger Arms SM-3	Sniper	NA	6 (Magazine)	6S2	4	4,000¥
Walther WA 2100	Sniper	NA	8 (Magazine)	6S2	4.5	6,500¥
Enfield AS7	Shotgun	3	10 (Clip)	4M3	4	1,000¥
Defiance T-250	Shotgun	4	5 (Magazine)	3M3	3	500¥
Mossberg CMDT	Shotgun	2	8 (Clip)	5M3	4.25	1,400¥
Mossberg CMDT/SM	Shotgun	2	8 (Clip)	5M3	4.5	1,900¥
Submachine Guns						
AK-97 SMG/Carbine	SMG	4	22 (Clip)	4M3	4	800¥
Beretta Model 70	SMG	3	35 (Clip)	4M3	3.75	900¥
Heckler & Koch HK227	SMG	4	20 (Clip)	5M3	4	1,500¥
Heckler & Koch S variant	SMG	5	16 (Clip)	5M3	3	1,200¥
Heckler & Koch MP-5TX	SMG	5	20 (Clip)	4M3	3.25	850¥
Ingram Smartgun	SMG	5	32 (Clip)	5M3	3.0	950¥
Sandler TMP	SMG	4	20 (Clip)	4M3	3.25	500¥
SCK Model 100 SMG	SMG	4	30 (Clip)	5M3	4.5	1,000¥
Steyr AUG-CSL SMG	SMG	4	40 (Clip)	4M3	3.5	*
Uzi III	SMG	5	16 (Clip)	4M3	2	600¥
Tasers						
Defiance Super Shock	Taser	4	4 (Magazine)	Special	2	1,000¥
Light Machine Guns						
Ares MP-LMG	LMG	NA	Belt 50 (Clip)	5S3	7.5	2,200¥
GE Vindicator Minigun	LMG	NA	Belt 50 (Clip)	5S3	15	12,500¥
Ingram Valiant	LMG	NA	Belt 50 (Clip)	5S3	9	1,500¥
Steyr AUG-CSL LMG	LMG	NA	40 (Clip)	6M3	5.5	*
Laser Weapon						
Ares MP Laser	'Sniper'	NA	20 (Pack)	12M8/6L4	30	2.5m¥
Heavy Weapons						
FN MAG-5 MMG	MMG	NA	Belt 50 (Box)	8S4/4M2	9.5	3,200¥
Heavy MG	HMG	Na	40 (Clip)	12S4/6M2	15	4,000¥
Medium MG	MMG	NA	40 (Clip)	8S4/4M2	12	2,500¥
Stoner-Ares M107 GPHMG	HMG	NA	Belt 40 (Clip)	12S4/6M2	12.5	5,200¥
Assault Cannon	Cannon	NA	20 (Clip)	10D4/5S2*	20	6,500¥
Panther Assault Cannon	Cannon	NA	22 (Clip)	10D4/5S2	18	7,200¥
Missile Launcher	—	NA	Belt —	by type	8	8,000¥

	Intelligence	Ammo	Damage	Weight	Cost
Missiles					
AVM	4	4 (Break)	12D8/6D4*	3	2,000¥
APM	3	4 (Break)	5M3	2	1,000¥
HEM	2	4 (Break)	4M4	2	1,500¥
Long Range SAM	4	4 (Break)	7D6/4M3*	1.5	2,200¥

*Vehicle Damage

AMMUNITION, PER 10 SHOTS

	Damage	Weight	Cost
Regular Ammo	—	.5	20¥
Explosive Rounds	+2 Staging	.75	50¥
Flechette Rounds	−1 Power, +1 Staging	.5	100¥
Firepower™ Ammo*	6M2	.5	35¥
APDS Ammo	+1 Power, -1 Ballistic Armor	.25	70¥
Gel Rounds	4L1 Stun	.25	30¥
Stun Round	4M4 Stun	1	100¥
Assault Cannon Ammo	10D4/5S2		
10 pack	—	1.25	450¥
Belt 100	—	12.5	4,250¥
Taser Dart	Special	.5	50¥
Taser Cartridge	Special	.5	100¥

*Heavy Pistol Only

CLOTHING AND ARMOR

	Concealability	Ballistic	Impact	Weight	Cost
Armor Clothing	10	3	0	2	500¥
Armor Jacket	7	5	3	2	900¥
Armor Vest	12	2	1	1	200¥
Vest With Plates	10	4	3	2	600¥
Secure Clothing	12	3	0	1.5	450¥
Secure Jacket	9	5	3	3	850¥
Secure Vest	15	2	1	.75	175¥
Secure Ultra-Vest	14	3	2	2.5	350¥
Secure Long Coat	10	4	2	2.0	650¥
Lined Coat	8	4	2	1	700¥
Form-Fitting Body Armor					
Level 1	—	2	0	.75	150¥
Level 2	15	3	1	1.25	250¥
Level 3	12	4	1	1.75	500¥

HEAVY ARMOR

	Concealability	Ballistic	Impact	Weight	Cost
Partial Suit	NA	6	4	10+Body	10,000¥
Full Suit	NA	8	6	15+Body	20,000¥
Light Security	NA	6	4	9+Body	7,500¥
Medium Security	NA	6	5	11+ Body	9,000¥
Heavy Security	NA	7	5	13+Body	12,000¥
Security Helmet	NA	1	2	—	250¥
Helmet	NA	1	1	—	200¥

LEATHER

	Concealability	Ballistic	Impact	Weight	Cost
Real	NA	0	2	1	750¥
Synthetic	NA	0	1	1	250¥

CYBERTECH

HEADWARE

	Essence Loss	Cost
Communications		
Chipjack	.2	1,000¥
Datajack	.2	1,000¥
Commlink-II	.3	8,000¥
Commlink-IV	.3	18,000¥
Commlink-VIII	.3	40,000¥
Commlink-X	.3	60,000¥
Crypto Circuit HD (1-4)	.1	(Level) x 10,000¥
(5-7)	.1	(Level) x 20,000¥
(8-9)	.1	(Level x 30,000¥
(10)	.1	(Level) x 50,000¥
Scramble Breaker HD (1-4)	.2	(Level) x 20,000¥
(5-7)	.2	(Level) x 40,000¥
(8)	.2	600,000¥
Radio	.75	4,000¥
Radio Receiver	.4	2,000¥
Telephone	.5	3,700¥
Ears		
Cyber Replacement	.3	4,000¥
Modification	.1	2,000¥
Cosmetic Modification	0	1,000¥
Hearing Amplification	.2	3,500¥
Damper	.1	3,500¥
High Frequency	.2	3,000¥
Low Frequency	.2	3,000¥
Select Sound Filter (Levels 1-5)	.2	(Level) x 10,000¥
Recorder	.3	7,000¥
Eyes		
Cyber Replacement	.2	5,000¥
Camera	.4	5,000¥
Cosmetic Modification	0	1,000¥
Vision Magnification		
Optical 1	.2	2,500¥
Optical 2	.2	4,000¥
Optical 3	.2	6,000¥
Electronic 1	.1	3,500¥
Electronic 2	.1	7,500¥
Electronic 3	.1	11,000¥
Rangefinder	.1	2,000¥
Flare Compensation	.1	2,000¥
Low-Light	.2	3,000¥
Retinal Duplication (illegal)	.1	50,000+¥
Thermographic	.2	3,000¥
INTERNALS		
Cortex Bomb (illegal)	—	500,000¥
Memory	Mp ÷ 100	Mp x 100¥
Datasoft Link	.1	1,000¥
Display Link	.1	1,000¥
Data Lock	.2	1,000¥
Data Filter	.3	5,000¥
Internal Voice Mask	.1	7,000¥
Program Enabler	.1	1,000¥
Sense Link	.2	300,000¥
Internal Transmitter	.6	80,000¥
Video Link	.5	22,000¥
Internal Transmitter	.4	4,500¥

Skill Software and Computer Media Libraries

	Cost
Knowledge	Mp x 150¥
Active skill	Mp x 100¥
Language	Mp x 50¥

BODYWARE

	Essence Loss	Cost
Dermal Plating		
Level 1	.5	6,000¥
Level 2	1	15,000¥
Level 3	1.5	45,000¥
Filtration Systems		
Air Rating ÷ 10		15,000¥ x Rating
Blood Rating ÷ 5		10,000¥ x Rating
Ingested Toxin Rating ÷ 5		10,000¥ x Rating
Fingertip Compartment	.1	3,000¥
Muscle Replacement		
(Maximum Level 4)	Level	(Level) x 20,000¥
Program Carrier	.2	25,000¥
Smartgun Link	.5	2,500¥
Cyber weapons		
Hand Razors	.1	4,500¥
Retractable Razors	.2	9,000¥
Hand Razors (Improved Blades)	NA	8,500¥
Spur	.1	7,000¥
Retractable Spur	.3	11,500¥
Limbs		
Simple Replacement	1	50,000¥
Cyber Limb	1	100,000¥
Increased Strength	—	+ (Level x 150,000¥)
Built-In Smartgun Link	.25	2,500¥
Built-In Device	—	x 4 Normal Cost
Cyber Guns		
Hold-Out Pistol	.15	250¥
Light Pistol	.35	650¥
Machine Pistol	.4	900¥
Submachine Gun	.6	1,800¥
Heavy Pistol	1.0	800¥
Shotgun	1.1	1,200¥
Skill Hardwires		
Level 1-4	.2 x Rating	Rating x 5,000¥
Level 5-8	.25 x Rating	Rating x 50,000¥
Level 9-10	.3 x Rating	Rating x 500,000¥
Skillwires		
Level 1–3	.1 x Level	Rating x 10,000¥
Level 4–6	.2 x Level	Rating x 100,000¥
Level 7–9	.3 x Level	Rating x 1,000,000¥
Vehicle Control Rig		
Level 1	2	12,000¥
Level 2	3	60,000¥
Level 3	5	300,000¥
Boosted Reflexes		
Level 1	.5	15,000¥
Level 2	1.25	40,000¥
Level 3	2.8	90,000¥
Wired Reflexes		
Level 1	2	55,000¥
Level 2	3	165,000¥
Level 3	5	500,000¥

Name:_____ **Street Name:**_____ **Sex:**_____

Race:_____ **Karma:**_____ **Archetype:**_____ **Lifestyle:**_____ **Money:**_____

SKILLS & LANGUAGES

Skill	Rating
_____	_____
_____	_____
_____	_____
_____	_____
_____	_____
_____	_____
_____	_____
_____	_____
_____	_____
_____	_____
_____	_____
_____	_____

ATTRIBUTES

PHYSICAL — Rating

Body: _____
Quickness: _____
Strength: _____

MENTAL

Charisma: _____
Intelligence: _____
Willpower: _____

SPECIAL

Essence: _____
(Magic): _____
Reaction: _____

ALLERGIES

Substance: _____
Severity: _____
Racial Adv: _____

CONDITION MONITOR

PHYSICAL **MENTAL**

Unconscious > Possibly dead. | < Unconscious, Further damage causes wounds

Seriously > Wounded. | < Seriously Fatigued.

Moderately > Wounded. | < Moderately Fatigued.

Lightly > Wounded. | < Lightly Fatigued.

Damage Modifiers

Damage	T#	Initiative
None	–	–
Light	+1	-1
Moderate	+2	-2
Serious	+3	-3

WEAPONS

Name	Concealability	Reach	Short	Medium	Long	Extreme	Ammo	Dmg. Code
_____	_____	_____	_____	_____	_____	_____	_____	__/__/__
_____	_____	_____	_____	_____	_____	_____	_____	__/__/__
_____	_____	_____	_____	_____	_____	_____	_____	__/__/__
_____	_____	_____	_____	_____	_____	_____	_____	__/__/__
_____	_____	_____	_____	_____	_____	_____	_____	__/__/__

CYBERWARE

_____ _____ _____

Type	Rating	Type	Rating		Type	Rating	Type	Rating
_____	_____	_____	_____	1	_____	_____	_____	_____
_____	_____	_____	_____	2	_____	_____	_____	_____
_____	_____	_____	_____	3	_____	_____	_____	_____
_____	_____	_____	_____	4	_____	_____	_____	_____
_____	_____	_____	_____	5	_____	_____	_____	_____
_____	_____	_____	_____	6	_____	_____	_____	_____

Defense Pool _____

Dodge Pool _____

Magic Pool _____

Astral Pool _____

ARMOR AND GEAR

_____ _____
_____ _____
_____ _____
_____ _____
_____ _____
_____ _____

STREET SAMURAI

VEHICLE

Type _____

Condition Monitor

Rating

Handling	_____
Speed	_____
Body	_____
Armor	_____
Signature	_____
Pilot	_____
Firmpoints	_____
Hardpoints	_____

< Vehicle Destroyed

< Serious Damage

< Moderate Damage

< Light Damage

Other Items

CONTACTS

_____
_____
_____
_____
_____
_____
_____
_____
_____
_____
_____
_____
_____
_____
_____

CHARACTER DRAWING

SPELLS

Type	Max Force	Staging	Drain Code
_____	_____	_____	___/___
_____	_____	_____	___/___
_____	_____	_____	___/___
_____	_____	_____	___/___
_____	_____	_____	___/___

CHARACTER NOTES

_____
_____
_____
_____
_____
_____
_____
_____
_____
_____
_____
_____
_____
_____

GEAR

_____ _____
_____ _____
_____ _____
_____ _____
_____ _____
_____ _____
_____ _____
_____ _____
_____ _____
_____ _____
_____ _____